D1505434

Officially Withdrawn

MAINSTREAMING EXCEPTIONAL CHILDREN

How To Make It Work

by

John A. Glover, Ph.D.
Tennessee State University
Nashville

and

Albert L. Gary, Ph.D.
University of Tennessee
Chattanooga

THE BOXWOOD PRESS

© 1976
by
The Boxwood Press

No part of this book may be reproduced in any form
without written permission of the Copyright owner.

ISBN: 0-910286-49-3

Distributed by:

THE BOXWOOD PRESS
183 Ocean View Blvd.
Pacific Grove, CA 93950

  408—375-9110

Printed in U.S.A.

9 4 7 0 1 0

Contents

Introduction

SINCE the early 1960's, "*Change!*" has been the battle cry of the new left, radicalized students, radicalized professors, angry parents, concerned educators, the promotors of Freedom and Dignity, and a host of other groups and splinter groups. And, indeed, some change has occurred within the educational establishment. But basic, fundamental educational policies at the decision-making level of local school systems have remained pretty much the same. Why is it that these new laws aimed at education of the "handicapped" are so important? What things are going to happen to make conditions in education different? Or, is this just a lot of "hoopla" that will get a lot of attention and just wither away when some new ideas come into vogue? There are sound reasons why this new move to educate the "handicapped" fairly and humanely is a permanent thrust, and why it is believed *not* to be just another bandwagon for people to jump on and then abandon for something else more attractive or with more "pizzazz."

The Law

First, and perhaps foremost, the changes proposed are the *law*. This is quite different from a state or local department of education *policy*. Policies are subject to change upon pressure of political expediency, economic conditions, or personal whim. Although laws are passed, amended, and repealed by the pressures of the first two factors above (and sometimes the third), the processes of enacting, amending, and repealing laws are much more deliberate, time-consuming and thoughtful procedures than those of policy-making. Second, the existence of the laws is widespread; 48 out of the 50 states now have such laws and are at various points in trying to implement them. This is a clear

1

indication of the scope of influence and the depth of thinking and planning that has entered into their passage. Although the legislation stems from a Supreme Court decision, and precedence for the decision is as basic as the Fourteenth Amendment, it (the legislation) is being passed by state legislatures. This makes the impact quite different than the federal legislation which created the very important titled monies programs. Requests for those programs had to originate with the local education agency. Many agencies have not obtained titled money due to lack of local expertise in writing grants, administrative inertia, or a general mistrust of anything connected to federal funds. The new "handi-capped" acts *require* that local plans be written, and as added insurance that they will be, *all* educational funds except those comprising the local contribution are withheld until an "approved" plan is submitted. In short, state legislatures have used the same tactic used by the federal agencies, with one variation: in the fed-eral programs, money was *offered* with strings attached; the new legislation *demands* a program and makes vital education money conditional to an approved program.

The impetus for the legislation being passed is different, also. In the past, federal policy and research findings promoted by leading universities provided much of the force necessary. The education of the "handicapped" acts, while taking their precedence from the aforementioned sources, were stimulated by and have received most of their support from the "grass roots" influence of parents of exceptional children and from leaders in the community who were concerned about local people and local children whom they know and see socially on a regular basis. While this may not seem important on the surface, the emotional component is highly significant in sustaining a movement, once it is established. A program that has been initiated as a result of research is not likely to have the wide-spread support of large numbers of people as one that began from what many parents believed to be cruel and unprofessional treatment of their children.

What Does it Require?

Typically, the new legislation requires that all students, kindergarten through grade 12, and all potential students (pre-school suspected deaf or hard-of-hearing down to age 3; any handicap ages 18 through 21) be screened for identification and possible verification of handicapping conditions, and for eligibility of supplementary educational services. In describing who is eligible for supplementary services, the legislators are careful to point out the inappropriateness of "labeling," such as "retarded," "emotionally disturbed," etc.; but at the same time, the labels are used to describe those students who are eligible. The preceding is just one of the semantic problems raised by the legislation. In most cases, guidelines issued by the state department of education officials have clarified the labeling issue. However, it still constitutes a problem for those school systems who persist in using traditional methods of student identification, and who have not adopted programs of identification based on educational rather than medical or psychometric factors.

Once the screening and identification of persons who are likely to be eligible for supplementary services is complete, the "suspected" must be verified. This process, too, is one that represents a vast departure from traditional verifications. A multidisciplinary team is required to make the final identification. In composition, the team is typically made up of the school principal, a person certified in one or more areas of special education (such as speech and hearing, learning disabilities, etc.), a classroom teacher, a guidance counselor and psychologist, and a *parent*. In practice, a more diverse and larger multidisciplinary team is appropriate for large school systems, and a smaller team (but still including a parent) is more akin to what one would find in a small, rural system. The multidisciplinary approach offers several very sound and practical advantages.

Whether a person is eligible for supplementary services is no longer a matter for only one person to decide. The school, the behavior exhibited by students in school, represents only a small part of an individual's total life. It is appropriate, then, that the child be viewed by a number of different people and from a number of different perspectives. When one individual, such as a school psychologist or a medical doctor, is charged with the responsibility of deciding who shall receive special services, the data that is collected and used to make the determination of eligibility is most often a function of the professional's "field" or area of greatest competence. Educators have come to know that while such information is sometimes useful, it is often incomplete.

Most of the new laws state that, in effect "... all children who are residents of .... be afforded a public education within the 'regular' classroom or within the 'regular' school complex, regardless of the nature of the child's social, emotional, intellectual, or environmental handicap...." The preceding is a big order, but it is one which must eventually be carried out. In the meantime, there are immense legal, financial, and administrative problems to be resolved. Most state legislatures have provided "due process" procedures to local school systems which are designed to see that each child receives the education to which he or she is entitled, and at the same time, to see that the local school systems are not beseiged with requests that they cannot fulfill without a good deal of planning, purchasing, and building. The legislatures have also provided formulas designed to make it possible to obtain the needed funds to purchase outside services, train teachers and other school personnel, rennovate buildings, and facilities and purchase newer and more appropriate educational materials and supplies which are geared to the student populations' disabilities.

While the state laws have provided the money to finance the educational innovations, and while guidance is given on methods of identifying eligible persons, and the desired consumer outcomes have been eloquently stated, long-standing procedural matters in the public school process and long-standing assumptions about the nature of teaching and evaluation are not dealt with at all. Some state departments of education have provided guidelines dealing with the above issues; others have not. In some instances, the guidelines are jealously guarded by a few persons at high administrative levels in local agencies. This has the effect of preserving the status quo—or at least making eduational change slow. In states where no guidelines are provided, the local education agency is left up to its own devices as to how to go about (or not, as the case may be) fulfilling the laws. The balance of this book articulates the various issues and changes that are brought about by passage of the new legislation, poses the modern against the traditional practices, and offers procedural methods that satisfy the intent of the laws with a minimum of disruption.

Chapter 1

What is *Mainstreaming?*

MAINSTREAMING is the term that has been used to describe the process of educating all students, regardless of their physical, psychological, intellectual, or environmental handicaps, along with non-handicapped students. Mainstreaming legislation has been passed in 48 of the 50 states, with full implementation required by most states no later than 1978.

The Education of the Handicapped Acts espouse a different set of values and assumptions about the handicapped student and the educational process than that of the traditional approach to education. One of the values has to do with the *worth* of an individual. The "Education of the Handicapped Acts" presume that *the worth of all human beings is the same* and that *the legal rights of the handicapped to a public education are intact,* without regard to the fact that providing education to the handicapped may be more expensive and require more teaching skills than that of the non-handicapped. It is acknowledged that the modern world is complex and dynamic, and as such, virtually everyone may be taught *to produce some product or render some service* valuable to the other members of the population, and through doing so, make it possible for virtually *everyone to feel a sense of worth as a human being.* It is no longer assumed that there is only one curriculum and one method of teaching it. Rather, it is presumed that not only must the curriculum be varied according to the characteristics of individuals, but the methods of teaching should also be marked by diversity.

The mainstreaming legislation all stems from the same Supreme Court decision, but takes its precedence from the Fourteenth

Amendment to the Constitution of the United States. The laws represent education's most valiant effort yet to make the public school process effective. The laws are rather straightforward in content: they are eloquent in stating "what" is to be done. It is the "how" that will prove to be troublesome to education unless many traditional procedures and assumptions are abandoned. Among the issues raised are these:

1. Who is handicapped?

2. How do we determine who is handicapped?

3. Does the "fault" always lie within the child (or, in fact, does it ever)?

4. Will group instruction be continued, or will instruction consist of group/individualized instruction, or will it be individualized entirely?

5. How will student performance be evaluated?

6. How will small, poor school systems deliver the esoteric services required by the laws?

7. How will teacher education programs be affected?

Basic Requirements of the Law

In addition to requirements regarding education of all students in the "regular" school program, what are the other provisions destined to affect handicapped students, their parents, the schools, and teacher training programs?

Student Identification

Most of the new state legislation has specific regulations regarding student identification procedures. The first step involves the screening of all students enrolled in school for medical, physical, psychological, educational and environmental handicaps. In addition to those students enrolled in school, all children 3 years old up to school age must be screened for hearing problems. Those identified must begin receiving services including hearing aids (where indicated) and/or speech and hearing therapy. The school systems must make a concerted effort to locate all persons up to 21 years of age who have not completed their elementary and/or high school education, and provide them the means of doing so if they so desire. During the initial screening process in which all children are surveyed, audiometric examinations and telebinocular visual examinations must be administered to all as a routine matter.

Criteria must be established by the local education agency whereby all students may be singled out who require more thorough medical, psychological, environmental, and educational evaluation before their educational programs are prepared. Specific procedures are given for the assessment process with these children.

The assessment process must not *end* with a diagnostic or categorical label attached to the child, as has been the traditional practice. Mainstreaming legislation strictly forbids the use of labels, and instead requires that a multifaceted assessment be conducted which ends with an *individual* educational program for each identified child.

Student identification ends with the student being "placed" in a program. In traditional practice, placement usually meant isolation from peers (age-group) and segregation with other students of a similar "diagnosis." Very often, it also meant removal from the regular school complex to a "special school" or to an institutional setting specializing in custodial-type care. Mainstreaming legislation makes these practices impossible except in instances when it is absolutely necessary, and then it is not seen as a terminal action. All placements, even those that are made outside the regular school complex, are seen as tentative and subject to constant on-going review. Rather than placement being described in terms of the setting to which the child is taken or in terms of the child's diagnostic category, it is described in terms of "option." Options describe the kinds and amounts of *instruction* the student receives.

Fault

Mainstreaming legislation does not presume that the "fault" lies within the child. Evidence of this is the provision that is made for teacher training. Positions are described, some of them new, that are required to properly implement the new practices of identification and teaching. Legislators and state department of education officials recognize that many of the skills described simply are non-existent at the local school level. But rather than try to bring in a large number of new personnel (even if they existed somewhere and it were possible to hire them), the legislation provides for the systematic training of existing personnel to fill the new positions and qualifications. Large amounts of money have been made available for tuition and stipends for those teachers and educational personnel who wish to upgrade their skills..

But teaching skills are not the only elements of the educational environment requiring modification. The Education of the Handicapped Acts will require the renovation of the interior and exterior of most existing school buildings. Many, if not most, of the existing educational structures were not designed with the physically handicapped in mind. There are typically not enough rest rooms, and existing rest rooms are not equipped for handicapped persons. The entrances are usually not wide enough for wheel chairs to enter. Wheel chairs also require ramps and curbs especially designed for them—both inside the buildings and on the grounds and approaches to the buildings. Legislation has provided for such renovations and requires any new buildings to be built to special new specifications.

In addition, the teaching of the handicapped (for whatever reason) requires instructional equipment and materials not found in the traditional school. The new legislation provides monies for the purchase of new materials, equipment, supplies, etc., that might be required in the instruction of the handicapped.

Parental Involvement

In most of the new legislation, there are two major provisions involving parents that are somewhat revolutionary: (1) Participation in the diagnostic process, and (2) the right to question or challenge the child's educational placement and program (or lack of it). A procedure called "due process" is outlined in the legislation, and must be made available not only to the parents of exceptional children, but to the public in general. It describes the appeal process, and takes the parent all the way to the point where civil action may be taken by the parent against the school system.

Required Plan

Each local school system is required to submit a plan of action to the state department of education for approval. The plan includes such facts as the number of handicapped children to be served, the kinds of materials, equipment, renovations, *personnel, and personnel skills* needed to properly serve the students. Local educational agencies must describe in *behavioral terms* the screening, assessment and placement process, and must specify how many children they have to serve by option. On-going individualized instruction and student evaluation must be described in the state plan. The plan is reviewed and either approved or disapproved by the state department of education. In the event the plan is disapproved, or if it is approved and then it is discovered that the local agency has not implemented it as proposed, the state department of education has the prerogative of withholding *all* state educational funds for the school year in question.

The due process procedure which involves the parents' approval and right to legal redress, and the prerogatives of the state plan involvement of the option of withholding state funds for non-compliance put real "teeth" into the new legislation. These two points, in addition to the fact that mainstreaming is *law* and not just *policy,* serves notice on the local educational agencies that educational reform must become a reality.

Behavioral Psychology

For too long education has languished in the prescientific era of psychology. It will no longer be possible for educators to fall back on the pre-scientific explanation of student behavior in terms of the students' intent. It will no longer be possible to get by with rosy reports and glowing descriptions of programs filled with the non-specific flowery language of the romantic poet. It is presently not popular to explain non-achievement of students in terms of their genetic inferiority. This is not to say that there are no children born whose genetic endowment does not permit them to achieve at the rate of certain other students. It is to say that when this is clearly the cause, it must be established without equivocation and not used as a way of avoiding the provision of quality instruction in a quality environment.

The new approach to education, perhaps without the full knowledge of the legislators, embraces the principles of *operant psychology* and the philosophy of *behaviorism.* For without the fifty-plus years of operant research and behaviorism, it would not be possible to implement the mainstreaming legislation. It is ironic that behaviorism, the purported enemy of "Freedom" and "Dignity," is the method by which millions of school children (many of them for the first time) will be afforded the status of fellow human beings. Whereas the concept of "Freedom" (when used in the traditional sense) is nothing more than a highly reinforcing belief, the concept of "Dignity" is not. The arrangement of the instructional contingencies along the lines suggested by the mainstreaming laws will verify the latter, especially for those parents and students who have been denied what has been legally theirs for some time.

Small and Poor Systems

Although the mainstreaming legislation is needed and appropriate, and although the funding of direct and indirect services is generous, and even though differential-position funding is providing teachers of the various student options in a progressive and equitable formula, there are many esoteric services that are not within the reach of many small school systems. A method will be discussed whereby school systems may band together for their mutual benefit, but still not lose the individuality and autonomy that small school systems guard so jealously.

Responsibilities of Higher Education

The passage of the mainstreaming legislation will profoundly affect not only the local educational systems and the way they "do business," but higher education, particularly teacher training programs, will be shaken to the very roots. One educator remarked after reading his state's version of the handicapped act, "It'll be five years before the dust settles!" There is no reason to doubt that his comment characterizes the commotion and activities the implementation of the laws will cause in higher education. State departments of education have become specific in their demands for educational services, and in turn, the local systems must be as specific in what they are providing. It will not be surprising at all when the local educational systems use their new-found skills in articulation to reject a large portion of what is now required for teacher certification, and to insist that universities provide teachers with many skills required by the new legislation that are not now being offered.

Chapter **2**

Screening and Assessment; What Are They?

SCREENING AND ASSESSMENT is a way of saying "diagnosis—and much, much more." There are many factors that affect
the effectiveness of educational programs, and among the most
important is the information you begin with, or the educational
diagnosis. We are concerned with three major items in arriving at
the educational diagnosis, hereinafter referred to as the screening
and assessment. They are: (1) the student as an organism, (2) the
student as having a history of reinforcement, and (3) the teacher
and the administration as arrangers of environmental contingencies.

As an organism, the student is endowed with a unique set of
genetic and somatic characteristics—that is—unless he or she is
an identical twin. With this exception, each student is literally "one
of a kind." As an organism, each student has a history of reinforcement that is peculiar to him or her, and this is true even for
identical twins. Most school systems have not yet recognized
these facts, and few have begun to design educational programs
with them in mind.

⚹ A Brief History

Before the advent of supplementary services to handicapped
students, many parents closeted their handicapped children away
from the public's eyes, and in many instances, mandatory education laws were not enforced on parents of the handicapped. Later
special schools were developed and parents began to send their
children to these residential facilities. The first facilities were for
the blind, the deaf, the retarded, and the emotionally disturbed.

The emotionally disturbed child whose behavior could not be controlled at school was allowed to remain at home. If the child's behavior could not be controlled at home, he or she was treated as an adult, that is, institutionalized along with adults. When supplementary services were introduced to public education, more often than not, the separation of students who displayed unusual physical or behavioral characteristics continued, but took on more subtle forms. Separation of the "normals" from the "non-normals" was justified on the assertions that the education of the "non-normals" would be more efficient if they could be taught in isolation with those of a similar diagnosis, where an individual trained especially for teaching that category of disability could work with them, and that their inclusion in classes or groups of "normals" would hamper the educational progress of the "normals." While there are elements of truth in both assertions, depending upon other conditions, the real problem had not been addressed: that of providing teachers with the appropriate teaching skills, and of arranging the environmental contingencies for the teachers to exercise the skill. Little or no thought was given to changing the instructional procedures to fit a diverse group of learners. Administrative efficiency, which demanded (or so it seemed) group-centered activities, took precedence over any individualized approach to instruction and evaluation.

Early diagnoses were usually medical, psychological, psychiatric, or some combination thereof. Most traditional diagnoses resulted in a descriptive formulation of the student that had little or no demonstrable connection to the child's academic functioning. Mental retardation was a psychometric diagnosis; emotional disturbance was a psychiatric diagnosis; neurological handicap was a physical-medical diagnosis. None of these designations led to the development of appropriate educational intervention strategies. Traditional diagnosis did a good job of labeling the individual but provided the teacher with no specific educational program to use with the child. The public has come to realize that labels per se are appropriate for jelly jars but are inappropriate for human beings.

Diagnosis came to mean "different;" "different" easily came to mean "unacceptable." The notion of unacceptability was reinforced by the separation of students to the basement, the boiler-room, or some other unorthodox classroom setting. Parents of exceptional children, civic leaders, concerned educators, and others became more and more vociferous in their demands for humane treatment of students as people. These formulations led to the development of diagnostic procedures that are more logically related to the goals of education.

Most of the new legislation either implies or directs the abolishment of a separate educational program for the handicapped; that is to say, all educational activities should be under one banner. The new focus is educational diagnostics, as opposed to psychological or medical diagnostics (to the exclusion of educational considerations). In combining special and regular educational programs and in requiring educational diagnosis, all children are to be screened and assessed for possible supplementary services.

What, then, are the criteria by which children should be evaluated in the process of determining who shall receive special services? Do we, indeed, look *only* at students while conducting screening and assessment activities? These two questions are fundamental and relate directly to the three general factors cited previously as being crucial to the implementation of the new legislation. In traditional educational settings, education has paid the most attention to the least accessible factor: that of genetic endowment. In the traditional methods of diagnosis for special educational needs, the standard IQ test has been relied heavily upon to single out those persons who are "in the most trouble" in the academic setting. Endowment, in the sense that it is meant in the first chapter, is something quite different and a great deal more than a set of standardized scores on an IQ test. By endowment, it is meant the general state of health and the degree of physical integrity of the individual, the abilities displayed which we generally call "intelligence," and the susceptibility of the individual as an organism to certain kinds of reinforcement. And the latter broadens considerably the scope of concern for the educational diagnostician. But, as noted before, these informations are not the most accessible, and hence, lack the precision we need to do something for a given individual.

The information that has the highest accessibility, the *specific behavior the individual emits* and the *conditions under which he or she does so,* has been given the least amount of attention. If this is not clear to the reader at this point, elaboration in later sections will clarify the matter. For now it is sufficient to say that teachers and administrators do not gather specific information about student behavior in the educational setting in a continuous and ongoing fashion. The information that is gathered is general, and focuses on groups of students rather than individuals. It is mostly confined to measurements taken at wide intervals. While the general and group information is appropriate as a starting point, it almost always suggests that one proceed further with a more specific process with certain individuals, and educators almost never do. The information-gathering process stops too soon, right at the threshold of the most available and informative data of all.

How, then, should the screening process begin? Since the first factor mentioned has to do with endowment (in the general sense as is operationally defined), perhaps all students should be viewed for both chronic and acute medical conditions. As a beginning, and because the legislation is concerned with "handicapped" students, we may confine our definition of "handicapped" to these criteria. However, as will be seen later, "handicapped" does not necessarily mean *only* physically handicapped, nor does it imply that the handicapping conditions always lie within the child.

Below is a form that may be used by any classroom teacher to record information that may be available from the cumulative record, the family of the child under consideration, or which may be obtained through a physical examination (if symptoms exist which suggest that such an examination is warranted).

In the traditional method, students who are identified by the above criteria would be classified as "special" students and might

STUDENT SCREENING—MEDICAL

Teacher: You will find some student medical classifications and physical descriptors and characteristics listed below. Please consult the child's cumulative folder and make observations, and check or fill in those blanks that are appropriate.

Observations

Unusually obese .... ☐

Unusually thin .... ☐

Unusually tall .... ☐

Unusually short .... ☐

Premature appearance of secondary sex characteristics ☐

Delayed appearance of secondary sex characteristics .... ☐

Does the student take medication regularly? ....yes/no

If so, what is it? ....
....

Dosage: ....

How often? ....

Medical

Heart disease .... ☐

Respiratory disease ....☐

Bone, joint, muscle disorder ☐

Gastrointestinal disorder .... ☐

Endocrine disorder .... ☐

Deaf or severe hearing loss . ☐

Blind or severe visual impairment .... ☐

Urinary disorder .... ☐

Any addictive condition? yes/no
....
....

List any behavioral side effect or admonition on student treatment recommended as a result of effects of medication. ....
....
....

possibly be placed in a "special" program. This is in spite of the fact that the information is very general, and in all cases is not sufficient to indicate that special help is even needed. In no case does it indicate what kind of special help should be provided, especially in certain chronic conditions that lack high visibility. Therefore, without gathering more specific information, a student could be "misclassified" in either direction. This leads to the next logical step in the assessment of students, that of the general academic evaluation. Below is a form some school systems use to identify those students who are "in trouble" academically.

Note: In the criteria for inclusion in special programs based on academic performance, those students who are two or more grade levels above or below the norm are designated. It is easy for most educators to accept the fact that an individual who is two or more grade levels *below* the norm should be given special help. However, it is sometimes difficult to convince some teachers and administrators that the child who is performing well above the norm might not be in the best possible program. The most frequent comment from teachers when such a student is identified is, ". . . well, that person is just a good student. . . ." What is meant by that is that the student does not cause trouble, learns quickly, and most probably, even with poor instruction. However, the fact that a student is performing well above the norm does not mean that he or she is in an appropriate program, and that determination cannot be made without more specific information.

So far we have looked only at the student, and in only a general way. This ignores the *environment* of the child, both at school and away. But the process described is probably a fairly reliable method of finding those students who should perhaps have special services. It stops short, however, of providing placement data and program content, instructional procedures and instructional materials, activities and evaluation methods. What has been described to this point are largely screening activities. Once screening is accomplished, we are fairly certain that the target population

STUDENT SCREENING—ACADEMIC

Student's Name.............................. Grade........ School...........................

Examining Teacher ....

Standardized Achievement Measures

Teacher: Please consult the child's cumulative folder and record the requested information. Please do not use data more than two calendar years old. If there is no data available, either in total or by category, leave the space(s) blank.

Areas	Grade Level When Tested	Standardized Test Grade Level	Years Above Grade	Below Grade	Stanine Rank (If shown)
Mathematics		comp. concepts prob. solv.			comp. concepts prob. solv.
Spelling					
Abstract Reasoning					
Reading Comprehension					
Vocabulary					
Science					

needing special help is somewhere in the group screened. But where are they, who are they, and what kind of information do we need to help them more efficiently? For that we turn to *assessment;* but before outlining the mechanics of assessment, it is appropriate to spend some effort in discussing the elements of a good screening and assessment plan.

The child and his or her teacher(s) co-constitute the *instructional environment,* each interacting with the other to evoke behavior that is reciprocal in nature. Thus, the aim of assessment is not to evaluate the child in a vacuum nor to automatically fix or manage the child. Rather, it is to evaluate the child as he or she interacts and is affected by the many environments in which he or she functions, and to find ways in which it will be possible to restructure those situations which evoke, perpetuate, or accelerate failure.

Within the broad statement of purpose above, any screening and assessment plan should encompass at least six components:

1. Primary prevention;

2. Multidisciplinary assessment;

3. Multifaceted assessment;

4. Behaviorally-oriented assessment;

5. Naturalistic assessment;

6. Continuous assessment.

Primary prevention is the aspect of the screening process which extends furthest beyond the school campus proper. In order to be properly prepared with personnel, facilities, materials and equipment, it is necessary, long before they enter school, to know who those students are and what their handicaps are likely to be. In addition to making preparation for the time when students will formally enter school, it is possible to work with parents, pediatricians, the departments of public health, and with public and private helping institutions to begin to render early, preventative service to handicapped students. The physically handicapped, the multi-handicapped, and especially those children who are destined to be diagnosed as "learning disabled" can be helped appreciably if they are provided special training during the preschool years. Early detection of certain disabilities make it possible to significantly influence later academic competencies when it is not possible to do so if the difficulties are not detected until the child's early and important developmental years have expired.

Multidisciplinary and *multifaceted* assessment both address themselves to the variability of behaviors of the perceiver and the perceived, and the variability of instruments, techniques, and methods designed to evaluate behavior. Behavior is not uniform across situations; the behavior of an individual varies directly with the history of reinforcement of the individual and the environmental contingencies operating in a given setting. Therefore, it is highly appropriate to use not only a variety of people (and hence, perspectives) in the evaluation process, but to use a number of different data-gathering procedures. Educational assessment is not the province of any one particular profession, just as the standardized instrument cannot yield enough information from which to formulate an educational program. For instance, a medical diagnosis may give accurate and reliable information about the state of health of a given individual at a particular point in time, but this alone is not enough information to tell a teacher exactly what and how to teach a child. Likewise, an intelligence test may yield clues as to the student's fund of knowledge and his or her ways of responding to various elements of the environment, but it is next to impossible to write educational programming from the results of such a test.

Behaviorally-oriented assessment is just what it appears to be: the gathering of observable, measurable behaviors that are relevant to the design of educational programs. Labels such as "retarded," "learning disabled," or "emotionally disturbed" are shorthand methods of describing clusters of typical behaviors which may be subject to wide interpretation, but which seem to aid in talking about the individual. Often people infer inaccurate and inappropriate characteristics about the individuals so labeled, and rarely do they know precisely what should be prescribed in the education of such persons. By focusing on behaviors that can be observed and measured, it is much easier to specify alternative behaviors and educational activities and conditions to bring them about.

Naturalistic assessment requires that data are collected in those settings in which the child lives and works rather than in an artificially contrived situation. In schools, psychological testing removes the child and the assessor's contact with the child's teachers, friends, and other persons important to the child's life. These people are thus isolated from the information-gathering process and the assessor is prevented from obtaining data concerning those events in the natural environment that may be evoking academic difficulty and those that may be sustaining it. Naturalistic assessment is direct assessment. It demands that behavior be viewed as it occurs in real life settings, not as it is deduced from test results. Direct measurement takes place at the site where behavior naturally occurs. To evaluate the child's academic functioning it is more valid to observe the child as he actually performs in the classroom than it is to interpret what his academic functioning might be in the class from intelligence or achievement tests.

Continuous assessment or evaluation is a dynamic process; it is on-going. Most academic measurement occurs only at infrequent intervals. Such measurement does not allow the teacher to monitor the instructional procedures so they can be redesigned for those children for whom they are not effective. Children may continue to have difficulty in comprehending material or executing academic performances within widely spaced assessments. Assessment that closely approximates continuous measurement ensures that the teacher can alter the material presented or restructure the instructional strategies more quickly. With the use of continuous measurement, there is less lapsed time between student difficulty, recognition of that difficulty, and intervention.

Although some psychologists, those of the behaviorist persuasion in particular, reject the importance of the so-called developmental skills in the assessment of the child, it seems as though assessments of students of grades K-4 should include an individual analysis of development. Developmental skills are those behaviors characteristic of children, by age groups, that are subsumed under gross and fine motor activities, social skills (including play activities and general interpersonal decorum), paper and pencil skills, characteristics of communication, and mathematical behaviors. Such analyses are usually conducted with a checklist or inventory that has been standardized at various age levels. "Good" items on such checklists are behaviorally stated, and ratings are expressed in "can do" or "cannot do" terms. Below is a sample form of developmental skills.

Developmental lists are given various weights in importance, depending on who is doing the evaluation. Some psychologists hold that students cannot begin to learn academic skills normally expected of their age group until they have mastered the developmental skills characteristic of their age group; there is evidence pro and con. One assumption is that the child as an organism is maturing and developing, and that poor performance or late performance of developmental skills indicate differences in endowment. The behaviorists would say that aside from medically-confirmed retardation and certain central nervous system disorders or birth defects, low or late developmental skills indicate an "underdeveloped" environment. One renowned behaviorist states that ". . . since internal states are almost exclusively conjectural, the only valid inference that can be made about a child's low developmental level is that the environmental contigencies are inhibiting (or at least not facilitating) learning."

Regardless of the theoretical position taken, a survey of developmental skills seems essential to a complete educational analysis,

STUDENT SCREENING—DEVELOPMENTAL

This Section for Grades K-2 and Special Education Self-Contained Classes.
Please check appropriate column:

I. COMMUNICATION

	Can Do	Can not Do
A. Language:		
Obeys simple instructions.	☐	☐
Understands orders containing: on, in, behind, under, above, in front of, on top, underneath.	☐	☐
Relates experiences in a coherent way.	☐	☐
Sentences contain plurals, past tense, "I," prepositions.	☐	☐
Comprehends simple questions and gives sensible answers.	☐	☐
Can define simple words.	☐	☐
Uses involved sentences containing: because, but, etc.	☐	☐
Can execute "triple order," e.g., Put this... then... and afterwards....	☐	☐
Can understand directions: upper left, bottom right, etc.	☐	☐
Can repeat a story without much difficulty.	☐	☐

B. Differences:

	Can Do	Can not Do
Can tell sex differences (e.g., man, woman, boy, girl).	☐	☐
Can discriminate colors by matching.	☐	☐
Differentiates between short, long, big, small, thick, thin.	☐	☐
Discriminates and names four or more colors without mistakes. . . .	☐	☐
Refers correctly to "morning" and "afternoon."	☐	☐
Tells "left" and "right" on himself (e.g., left arm, right ear).	☐	☐
Names the days of the week and recognizes some days.	☐	☐
Understands differences between: day—week, minute—hour, etc. . .	☐	☐
Tells the time to a quarter of an hour.	☐	☐
Tells the time and associates time on clock with various actions and events.	☐	☐

C. Number Work:

	Can Do	Can not Do
Can differentiate correctly between one thing and many things.	☐	☐
Understands the difference between two and many things.	☐	☐
Can count mechanically ten objects.	☐	☐
Can handle "number situations" up to four (including "taking away").	☐	☐
Can arrange objects in order of size from the smallest to the largest.	☐	☐
Can count mechanically thirty or more objects.	☐	☐
Can handle "number situations" up to 13 or more (including "taking away").	☐	☐
Can recognize coins of various denominations up to a quarter.	☐	☐
Adds coins of various denominations up to a quarter.	☐	☐
Can give change out of a quarter.	☐	☐

D. Paper and Pencil Work:

Holds pencil and can imitate vertical and circular strokes. . . . . ☐ ☐
Can copy circles. . . . . ☐ ☐
Draws primitive "man" showing head and legs. . . . . ☐ ☐
Draws recognizable "men" and "houses." . . . . ☐ ☐
Prints his name and recognizes it among other printed
    words and names. . . . . ☐ ☐
Can recognize 40 or more words of everyday
    functional vocabulary. . . . . ☐ ☐
"Writes" his name (in script). . . . . ☐ ☐
Reads simple instructions, e.g., on public transport
    (besides functional vocabulary. . . . . ☐ ☐
Addresses envelopes in an acceptable manner. . . . . ☐ ☐
Reads simple printed matter, e.g., radio and t.v. guide. . . . . ☐ ☐

II. SOCIALIZATION

A. Play Activities:

Plays *in company* with others, but does not yet
    cooperate with others. . . . . ☐ ☐
Waits "his turn," can "share" at times. . . . . ☐ ☐
Plays cooperatively with others. . . . . ☐ ☐
Enjoys entertaining others. . . . . ☐ ☐
Plays competitive games, e.g., hide and seek, tag, etc. . . . . ☐ ☐
Acts out stories he has heard. . . . . ☐ ☐
Sings, dances to music, plays records. . . . . ☐ ☐
Plays simple table games, e.g., tiddly winks, dominoes, etc. . . . . ☐ ☐
Plays simple ball games with others, e.g., passing ball. . . . . ☐ ☐
Plays cooperative team games. . . . . ☐ ☐

III. MOTOR CONTROL

A. Dexterity (Fine Finger Movements):

Can string large beads. . . . . ☐ ☐
Can unscrew lids with a twisting movement or
    turn door knobs. . . . . ☐ ☐
Can cut paper with scissors. . . . . ☐ ☐
Can make constructive use of plastics,
    building blocks, etc. . . . . ☐ ☐
Can cut out pictures, though not very accurately. . . . . ☐ ☐
Can wind thread fairly evenly onto a spool. . . . . ☐ ☐
Can build elaborate structures with suitable
    materials (bricks, construction kits, etc.). ☐ ☐
Can cut cloth with scissors. . . . . ☐ ☐
Can pile papers, playing cards, etc., in a neat way. . . . . ☐ ☐
Can cut very accurately around outlines. . . . . ☐ ☐

B. Agility (Gross Motor Control):

Can kick ball without falling. .... ☐ ☐
Can jump with both feet. .... ☐ ☐
Can stand "tip-toe" for 10 seconds. .... ☐ ☐
Can skip on both feet. .... ☐ ☐
Boys use hammer correctly, girls begin sewing. .... ☐ ☐
Can throw ball and hit target (1'x1') 1½ yds. away. .... ☐ ☐
Uses "playground" apparatus in fairly "safe" and assured
     manner (swing, see-saw, ropes, etc.). .... ☐ ☐
Uses tools, kitchen utensils, garden tools. .... ☐ ☐
Can balance on "tip-toe" while bending forward. .... ☐ ☐
Can balance on "tip-toe" in crouched position. .... ☐ ☐

if for no other reason than the fact that developmental behaviors are a part of the individual's total behavior repertoire. The effect of such a survey is to focus attention on lack of skills, which can and should lead directly to special instructional objectives, to medical attention or to some other kind of combination of intervention. In any event, the child's chances of educational enhancement are strengthened.

It is also important to conduct surveys on behaviors associated with learning disabilities. Whether one is behaviorist or not, it must be admitted that many youngsters are born with (inherit) or acquire via prenatal or postnatal insult, damaged or malfunctioning afferent or efferent systems, or other structural or functional anomalies. Although the "true" source or etiology of such symptoms is not readily accessible, as has been pointed out earlier, it is still useful in that it focuses attention on the child's performances or behaviors and prompts the diagnostician and/or teacher to revise the environmental contingencies. Symptomatic information is inferential in nature, and may indicate endowment anomalies, inappropriate histories of reinforcement, poorly designed instruction in the present, or some combination of the foregoing. The precise etiology of the behavior is not necessarily crucial to know; the design of the instructional situation and the manipulation of the learning consequences, of course, *are* important. In certain instances, as with hearing loss or deafness and of correctable visual problems, etiology of behavior via precision diagnostics are of paramount importance. When symptoms of visual and auditory impairment are present, thorough hearing and visual diagnoses are in order. Below is a form that is widely used as a screening device for possible learning disabilities. It is not a diagnostic instrument, but is a checklist that will more than likely identify those children who should be given a more specific evaluation. A good rule of thumb is to sum the scores by each of the five main categories and divide the sums in each category by the number of items in that category. All students with scores of 3.5 or greater should be referred for further diagnosis.

STUDENT SCREENING
Learning Disabilities

Teacher: Read carefully the symptoms of disabilities which are listed. Score the child on a scale from 1 to 5; circle the appropriate score at the end of each statement.

Never 1
Seldom 2
Occasionally 3
Frequently 4
Always 5

SYMPTOMS OF DISABILITIES
I. VISUAL:

A. Rubs eyes. 1 2 3 4 5
   Complains that he can't see. 1 2 3 4 5
   Holds book close. 1 2 3 4 5
   Bumps into things. 1 2 3 4 5

B. Looks at end of word and guesses by minimal
     clue or combines end and beginning. 1 2 3 4 5
   Has difficulty finding key words. 1 2 3 4 5

C. Moves head instead of holding head
     still and moving eyes. 1 2 3 4 5

D. Loses place. 1 2 3 4 5
   Uses finger to point. 1 2 3 4 5
   Skips or re-reads lines. 1 2 3 4 5
   Needs a marker below line to keep place. 1 2 3 4 5

E. Holds book too close or too far away. 1 2 3 4 5
   Tends to move book closer on difficult words. 1 2 3 4 5
   When copying from board experiences blurring
     of print or watering eyes. 1 2 3 4 5

II. AUDITORY

A. Has weak or overloud voice. 1 2 3 4 5
   Breathes through mouth. 1 2 3 4 5
   Frequently needs oral directions repeated. 1 2 3 4 5
   Holds head on side. 1 2 3 4 5
   Watches speakers' lips. 1 2 3 4 5

B. Exhibits poor speech production. 1 2 3 4 5
   Exhibits poor spelling and phonic skills. 1 2 3 4 5
   Has difficulty distinguishing sameness or
     difference of sounds. 1 2 3 4 5

C. Has difficulty in auditory memory. 1 2 3 4 5
    Responds inaccurately to oral directions or questions. 1 2 3 4 5
    Is frustrated when asked to repeat a sequence from memory. 1 2 3 4 5

D. Cannot determine from which direction a sound comes. ... 1 2 3 4 5

E. Daydreams. 1 2 3 4 5
    Is inattentive. 1 2 3 4 5
    Is anxious. 1 2 3 4 5
    Has difficulty responding to oral directions,
        lectures, and conversations. 1 2 3 4 5
    Exhibits poor listening comprehension. 1 2 3 4 5

F. Forgets oral directions. 1 2 3 4 5
    Has difficulty finding words when speaking
        in front of class. 1 2 3 4 5
    Confuses labels. 1 2 3 4 5

III. VISUAL—Perceptual

A. Confuses words that look familiar. 1 2 3 4 5
    Has difficulty with all symbols. 1 2 3 4 5

B. Is inattentive. 1 2 3 4 5
    Is disorganized. 1 2 3 4 5
    Has problem with complex words. 1 2 3 4 5
    Has trouble reading small or different
        type or noting details. 1 2 3 4 5
    Writes poorly. 1 2 3 4 5

C. Confuses letters such as d and b or m and w. 1 2 3 4 5
    Changes sequence of letters within a word. 1 2 3 4 5
    Prints poorly. 1 2 3 4 5

D. Cannot recall newly learned words. 1 2 3 4 5
    Spells poorly. 1 2 3 4 5
    Writes poorly. 1 2 3 4 5

IV. VERBAL

A. Exhibits nasal sound production. 1 2 3 4 5
    Exhibits tremorous sound production. 1 2 3 4 5
    Exhibits husky sound production. 1 2 3 4 5
    Exhibits strained sound production. 1 2 3 4 5

B. Exhibits speech substitutions or omissions. 1 2 3 4 5
    Lisps. 1 2 3 4 5
    Exhibits shy or immature discrimination. 1 2 3 4 5
    Has problems in spelling and phonics. 1 2 3 4 5

C. Exhibits vocabulary and speech appropriate
        for much younger child. 1 2 3 4 5

D. Has incorrect or confused speaking vocabulary. 1 2 3 4 5
   Exhibits poor reading comprehension. 1 2 3 4 5
   Has difficulty following directions or
      using reading for study. 1 2 3 4 5
   Is inattentive. 1 2 3 4 5

E. Reverses sounds or words, for instance, says— "emeny"
      for "enemy," "log back" for "back log." 1 2 3 4 5
   Gets the facts but can't organize them. 1 2 3 4 5
   Has difficulty with blending in spelling or phonics. 1 2 3 4 5

F. When asked to speak is self-conscious. 1 2 3 4 5
   When asked to speak avoids participation. 1 2 3 4 5
   When asked to speak is nervous. 1 2 3 4 5
   When asked to speak is tense. 1 2 3 4 5
   When asked to speak is restless. 1 2 3 4 5
   When asked to speak has facial tic. 1 2 3 4 5
   When asked to speak shows displeasure through
      facial expression. 1 2 3 4 5

G. Is unable to name objects. 1 2 3 4 5
   Is unable to express himself verbally. 1 2 3 4 5

V. GROSS AND FINE COORDINATION

A. Confuses b and d. 1 2 3 4 5
   Reverses words. 1 2 3 4 5
   Displays inability to align numbers, words, objects,
      or horizontal or vertical planes. 1 2 3 4 5

B. Confuses left-right directions. 1 2 3 4 5
   Uses finger to keep place on page. 1 2 3 4 5
   Confuses beginning and ending of words. 1 2 3 4 5

C. Has difficulty with reading fluency. 1 2 3 4 5
   Has difficulty with writing. 1 2 3 4 5
   Is awkward. 1 2 3 4 5
   Is unable to skip or jump rope. 1 2 3 4 5

D. Grips pencil awkwardly. 1 2 3 4 5
   Shows tremor in writing. 1 2 3 4 5
   Has difficulty reproducing designs. 1 2 3 4 5
   Has difficulty reproducing letters. 1 2 3 4 5

E. Is slow and labored in body movements. 1 2 3 4 5
   Has difficulty sustaining a movement. 1 2 3 4 5
   Exhibits poor rhythm in writing. 1 2 3 4 5

To this point we have provided some "common sense" and fairly typical methods of conducting a screening process to determine who should be assessed in a more formal way for eligibility for special instructional services. We have suggested that standardized tests of achievement be used to determine in a general way, who those students are who are significantly ahead or behind the norm in achievement. We have indicated that it might be important in grades K-4 to survey each child's developmental or readiness skills. We have maintained that each child who displays symptoms of visual or hearing impairment should have an audiometric examination and/or a binocular visual test. A symptom checklist of behaviors indicative of learning disabilities is recommended to be administered to all those students who are well behind the norm of their class in achievement.

Many students display behaviors in the class, on campus, and in the general environment that may indicate social maladjustment, emotional disturbance, or behaviors that may be disruptive to their and/or other's learning. Certainly, a good screening form and a description of how to use it in the analysis of behavior is recommended for persons who must conduct screening and assessment. In gathering such specific behavior we have begun to move from the general to the particular, and from the least accessible to the most accessible information about a given child. A behavioral psychologist generally separates data-gathering into individual and group data. We will treat individual data first and then demonstrate the similarities and changes necessary to gathering appropriate group data.

Individual Data

The first step in gathering behavioral data for any individual is to concretely, specifically, and correctly define the behavior in question. The reason for this is that you or the person observing the behavior, must know when the behavior has occurred. For example, let us examine out-of-seat behavior. Is it necessary that a student step away from the desk, or is a lack of contact between the student's buttocks and the seat of the chair to be considered out-of-seat behavior? As you can see, without a good definition, the problem of identifying a behavior can soon get out of hand. For the purposes of our example we will consider any instance of lack of contact between buttocks and the seat of the chair as out-of-seat behavior. This does not answer all of our problems as we shall see later, but it does get us started in the right direction.

Let us look in on a hypothetical student that has come to be a source of concern to us because of his out-of-seat behavior. This student has become such a concern, in fact, that we intend to do something about his behavior. The first step in any behavior-change program is always the gathering of baseline data, i.e., the level of behavior before any treatment, the behavior under "natural" conditions.

Looking at the figure on page 33, which represents our hypothetical student's behavior, we see that the student was out-of-seat quite a number of times. The problem here, is how long an out-of-seat episode must be to count as out-of-seat? Does an incidence of ten minutes duration count the same as one of ten seconds? There are many different possible solutions to such problems, but we recommend a time-interval assessment in which the student's behavior is checked at certain intervals (every ten seconds, every minute, every thirty seconds) and his current behavior at each of these intervals is recorded. This eliminates the problems of differing lengths of behaviors fitting the same definition. This process has some drawbacks, however, it is almost necessary that an independent observer be present in the classroom. A teacher could, with great difficulty keep accurate time checks and behavior counts, but it seems that the teacher's effectiveness would be greatly impeded. The checklist would consist of nothing more than the kinds of behaviors under scrutiny spelled out on the left margin with the times noted across the top of the sheet (see figure, page 33).

A Record of One Student's Out-of-seat Behavior

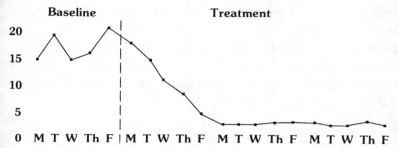

Out-of-seat behavior was determined by a time-interval assessment in which the behavior was noted in ten-second intervals.

A Checklist for Behavior

	8:00:00	8:00:10	8:00:20	8:00:30
Out-of-seat				
Hitting				
Time-off-task				
Social behavior; inappropriate				

A typical time schedule checklist usually is designed for the duration of some period, e.g., one hour.

Following the baseline data, while the treatment procedure is in effect, the same kind of data-gathering process is put into effect to determine if the treatment has had an effect. This is also pictured in the figure on page 33.

One to several different kinds of behaviors may be assessed in this manner. The only limiting factor is the capability of the data recorder and the fact that most treatments are designed to change one or two behaviors at a time.

Group Data

The process of gathering group data is very similar to that of individual data. Problems involved are the necessity for dealing with only one or two behaviors at a time, a greater number of observers to facilitate an adequate check of behavior, and the lack of precision that will inevitably occur. There are several different ways in which group data may be recorded, but we suggest a compilation of mean levels of behavior of the students with the use of several observers consecutively observing different students. Such a diagram is pictured in the figure on page 34.

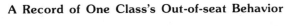

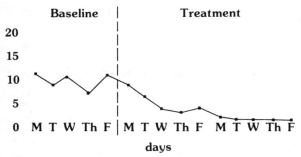

A Record of One Class's Out-of-seat Behavior

Out-of-seat behavior was determined by a mean score of all student's behaviors for each day. Behavior was noted consecutively by three observers for all students in ten-second intervals.

A comprehensive screening and placement program includes not only information about the students, but must also give information about the books, materials, equipment, facilities, and general environment of the school, and must include relevant information about how the student interacts with the teacher(s) and the typical behaviors of teachers. The screening process is more aptly directed at the student only. The analysis of the physical environment and the behavior of teachers is best analyzed at the point of preparation of the instructional objectives, implementation of the objectives, and at the point of academic evaluation of the student. Therefore, the presentation of these parts of the screening and assessment will be deferred until after the multidisciplinary team-members' qualifications, roles, and functions are described.

Chapter **3**

The Multidisciplinary Team: Who Does the Work?

IN ADDITION to bringing handicapped and non-handicapped students together in the "regular" classroom, mainstreaming requires that regular instructional personnel and the traditional special educators (and their professional support personnel: the psychologist, the psychometrist, the medical evaluator) work together. One of the problems experienced by the traditional educator is the communication gap that exists between the various professionals working with the same child. Often, different language is used to describe the same symptoms, disabilities that are the same are ascribed different causalities, and most troublesome: a hiatus usually exists between the description of what is wrong and what to do about it. The psychologist, for example, has typically not attempted to write educational programs, but has instead given a general description of a few types of instructional activities that might be productive. In some instances the psychologist has maintained that *identification* is the province of the psychologist, and that instructional goals, activities and materials should be provided by the teacher. The special education specialist is typically well qualified in methods and materials for specific disabilities, but traditional educational practices have kept the special educator short on diagnostic-test administration skills (this is the province of the psychologist). The traditional "regular" education program has discouraged the interaction of the traditional teacher, the special educator and the psychologist with regard to educational programming. The rationale has been if the child is a special-education child, a special educator should do the teaching. Clearly, what is needed is a combination of educational diagnostics, educational programming and instruction that can be administered by the regular classroom teacher. It is also clear that all this must take place (or as much as possible) at the interface of the teacher and the child. Any educator also knows that the foregoing is an impossible order for one person to fill. Conditions must be created such that the right professionals work with the child without drawing the professional boundaries so rigidly.

Another troublesome area in the assessment and placement procedure is that traditional practices do not allow the parent or the guardian of the child to participate in the determination of what data are to be collected, where the child will be placed, and the nature of the child's program. Here the medical profession has, perhaps unwittingly, been an accomplice in keeping the parents of exceptional children from knowing specifically what is being provided their children via special programs. It is traditional that the medical profession in the United States has been cloaked with a kind of mantle of omniscience; it has almost been Deified. School administrators have been keenly aware of this fact, and have used the medical report or medical pronouncement of "student condition" as a justification for placing a student in a given program. It is rare when a parent objects to a student being placed in a program with the evidence for placement being a medical doctor's report. While this is in no way an indictment of physicians, nor is it recommended that doctor's reports not be obtained if it is indicated, it is suggested that the involvement of a profession that is sacrosanct not only allows placement to occur in an orderly fashion, but causes most parents to have great confidence in the program in which the child is being placed. The fact of the matter is, few doctors know anything at all about the nature of the instructional procedures employed with students they have diagnosed and recommended for placement. What's more, the vast majority of doctors would not be qualified to render sound evaluation of such programs, even if they had intimate and detailed information about the procedures and content. The main point being made is that with the probabilities of accountability removed via the involvement of the medical doctor in special placements, school administrators have a golden opportunity to deliver second-class instructional service. These opportunities must be removed. Therefore, parents should be a part of the diagnostic, assessment, and placement procedures, and should have at least some veto power or redress procedure. Hence, parents are members of the multidisciplinary team.

In an ideal situation, members of the multidisciplinary team are as follows:

1. The referring teacher.

2. The consulting teacher.

3. The resource teacher.

4. The school principal.

5. The school counselor.

6. The school nurse.

7. The parent(s).

8. Ad hoc member(s).

In small schools and small school systems, there will be instances in which there is no school nurse and/or no school counselor. There *must* be a consulting teacher and a resource teacher(s), in addition to the school principal, the referring teacher, and the parent(s) or guardian of the child. Mainstreaming legislation requires that all the aforementioned interact in the determination of the nature of the child's assessment. Ad hoc members are those persons from any aspect of the child's environment who can contribute information that would aid in the preparation of the best educational program possible for the student.

The *referring teacher* initiates the screening and assessment process by gathering achievement data, developmental data, medical data from the cumulative folder, and making the recommendation that the child be evaluated for possible placement in a program of special study. Once the screening data are gathered and submitted to the multidisciplinary team, the referring teacher's responsibilities are largely over with respect to that child until it is time to implement the special program (presuming a program is eventually written and the student is placed in one of the "classroom" options). It is at this point that mainstreaming requires many of the traditional practices be dropped. In a traditional situation, the classroom teacher would make a referral, the psychologist would conduct an evaluation and write a report. The student might or might not be given a medical evaluation. The end result would be that the classroom teacher would be furnished a report or reports confirming what he or she already knew or strongly suspected about the child. There would be no specific educational program provided for the teacher, and hence, the teacher would be no better off than when the process was initiated. More important, the child would not have profited.

In the mainstreaming screening and assessment practices, the teacher provides the justification for conducting the assessment. The referring teacher becomes a part of the multidisciplinary team for the occasion of that child's assessment, but more as an observor than as a person contributing diagnostic data. The teacher is there to observe the data as they are gathered, the educational program that is formulated, and try to learn how to implement the program (if it is within his or her province). The teacher, therefore, is charged with rather heavy instructional responsibilities under mainstreaming (within certain "options"), but is relieved of making final diagnoses, writing highly specialized and individualized instructional objectives, and of the selection of esoteric materials and equipment of which he or she may not have special knowledge.

The *principal*'s function as the chief executive of the school is not greatly modified by service on the multidisciplinary team. In addition to the normally prescribed duties of principal, the shool's chief administrative officer must be responsible for informing all personnel of their duties in carrying out the mainstreaming requirements. The principal must continually monitor to see that each identified child is being attended, and must inform the parents of exceptional children of their rights under due process. It is recommended that the principal organize and develop a presentation consisting of narrative, colored slides, overhead projector, transparencies, and other related visual aids, showing each aspect of the special law's implementation. The presentations should be made at PTA meetings, general school meetings, and should be provided to local media. The principal is responsible for securing the permission of parents and guardians of children to be assessed and placed in the mainstreaming program. "Due process" provides a step-by-step procedure for those parents who disagree with the school's recommendations. "Due process" will be presented in a later section.

The *resource teacher* is a person who is trained, in the traditional sense, in one or more areas of student exceptionality, such as mental retardation, speech and hearing, or the learning disabled. Properly trained resource teachers have much knowledge of diagnostics and of methods and materials which generalize in use from one area of exceptionality to another, and ordinarily have some experience with a number of student exceptionalities. However, most state departments of education do not recognize the resource teacher as being qualified to make diagnoses. In traditional practice, the *special education teacher*'s work usually begins after the diagnosis is made—even though the diagnosis of the professional, in many cases, is not any more accurate than that which the special education teacher might have made. The practice of having *one* professional, such as the M.D. or Ph.D. psychologist, make the diagnostic pronouncement has severe limitations. One of them is the distorted worth of the program, as seen by members of the general public, via the close association of the medical profession to the placement procedure. The six components of the ideal screening and assessment program discussed in an early section illustrate most of the other limitations. Under mainstreaming, the resource teacher becomes a member of the multidisciplinary team, providing whatever expertise he or she can to the determination of what kind of data to collect, what kind of program to set forth for the child, and what kinds of materials and methods to use in the execution of the program. A more precise definition of the role of the resource teacher will be provided in the section covering "options."

There is no doubt that the *consulting teacher* is a key person in the proper implementation of the mainstreaming legislation. It is this person that is to remove much of the programming load from the classroom teacher. The consulting teacher not only has the skills necessary to be certified as a school psychologist, but must also be able to gather data and use them to formulate specific programs—the latter being a task the psychologist has not been able to do in the traditional situation. In addition to having the test administration, test interpretation and clinical skills of the psychologist, the consulting teacher must have thorough knowledge of instructional methods and materials for exceptional children, and enough medical training to know when it is necessary to collect and utilize medical information.

Currently, there are few, if any, colleges of education providing specific programs designed to train consulting teachers. It is the opinion of the authors that the consulting teacher's program should be interdisciplinary in nature. It is believed that if consulting-teacher training-programs are established within a traditional department, whether it be education, special education, psychology, or counselor education, that the graduates will generally have the same stereotypic views and explanations of behavior the programs should be designed to circumvent. "Hardening of the categories" is a serious affliction of many professional schools. It is proposed that the consulting teachers' required courses be determined by the competencies required of the position, and that the trainees be afforded the opportunity of taking the courses wherever they may be found in the university. In many instances, courses already provided in the catalogs of departments of education, special education, and psychology fit with the needs for consulting-teacher training. However, there are some skills that are best "lifted" from several traditional courses and some skills that are presently not being taught at some universities which should be organized into competency-based courses especially for the consulting teacher. The following is a survey of the instructional areas and general competencies derived from them which are believed to be essential to the basic program of the consulting teacher. Counseling, developmental psychology, and learning theory are those areas of instruction which usually have courses already in the catalog relevant to the consulting teacher. Diagnostics is an area that probably should be "lifted" from other professional departments (including both psychology and education). Individual programming and instruction is seen as a terminal part of the consulting-teacher's program, and one which will probably have to be completely organized by the consulting-teacher program-director. It should be as interdisciplinary as is possible, drawing from psychology, education, special education, pre-medical, counseling, sociology, etc. Because of the legal responsibilities of the school principal, he or she should serve as the administrative head of the multidisciplinary team. However, the consulting teacher must be the "working leader" of the team, and as such, should have the final responsibility for making the determination of what data to collect, what data to use, and when to ask for diagnostic help outside the professional areas of the team members' expertise.

Many schools do not have counselors at the elementary level, and there are still some schools with no counselors at the junior high and high school levels; however, the latter is the exception rather than the rule. Those systems that employ counselors (at any level) will clearly have an advantage in implementing the mainstreaming laws. Counselors are required to have varying amounts of training in the administration and interpretation of standardized tests. In situations where the counselors, the resource teacher, and the consulting teacher all have had training in testing, the formal diagnostic process will be greatly expedited. In addition to helping with individual and group testing, the counselor can also work with the principal in communicating with parents concerning the collection of data on referred students' behavior at home, in assisting parents in reviewing the placement data on their children, and in securing parental agreement on their children's program and placement. Most counselors should have at least the rudimentary elements of operant theory in their repertoires, and should be able to assist in the collection of behavioral data in the classrooms. The efficient collection and analysis of behavioral data is essential to providing individual programming, and those counselors who are trained in behavior modification can be invaluable to the multidisciplinary team efforts. As a member of the multidisciplinary team, the counselor should contribute a number of skills that do not overlap with those of the principal, their resource teacher, and the consulting teacher. A more specific role for the counselor will be discussed in a later section under "options."

One of the important principles underlying multidisciplinary assessment is the gathering of data from a number of sources. Parents can and should be persuaded to serve in an information-gathering capacity as often as is possible. There are other reasons for parental involvement than the need for variable source data, the most significant being that it is *their* child who is being assessed for placement in a special program, not some stranger. Contrary to what has been the practice in the past, each parent does have the right to help determine the nature of his or her child's educational program. In addition, the school systems should capitalize on the parents' special knowledge of their children. Many parents of exceptional children are amazingly well-informed on student exceptionalities—especially the exceptional category of their child. Special-education children are so different in their learning styles that it is difficult to maximize their success without information from the home environment and without parents aiding in the instructional efforts. Most parents of exceptional children want desperately to help their children and many are frustrated because they do not know what to do (or school systems have made them fearful of intervention at home). While in many instances parents of such children don't have sufficient training or lack the objectivity to provide instruction at home, it would serve the school systems (and the children) well if training and advice, along with special materials and equipment, could be provided parents for home instruction. By teaching parents how to help in the selection of materials, the methods of instruction, and by providing them with instructional programs, the teacher's job is made easier, the child's learning is enhanced, and the parents feel they are making a valuable contribution to their children's development. For those parents who unjustifiably feel guilt over their children's problems in learning, participation in their children's educational programs is extremely therapeutic.

An *ad hoc member* is a person, anyone, who may be able to contribute data important to the formulation of the child's educational program. Ad hoc members may be bus drivers, cafeteria workers, the neighbor, the postman, and virtually any other person in fairly regular contact with the child being assessed. Ad hoc members are multidisciplinary team members for that particular child's assessment, and may not necessarily serve as a member again. However, no restrictions are imposed on the number of individual assessments on which an ad hoc member may serve. Ad hoc members may be selected by a parent or any other team member, and selection should be based primarily on the basis of the person's regular interaction with the child in some capacity. It is most likely, however, that the child is the most important person to consult with regard to the selection of an ad hoc member. A simple question such as, "Who do you like a lot who might be able to tell us things you like to do and things that you are good at doing?" will often reveal an adult or a peer that has intimate information about the student's interests and capabilities, and about histories of reinforcement that might otherwise be a long time forthcoming. A word of caution on ad hoc members: it is wise to take care not to convey to an ad hoc member that his purpose is to "snoop" or to "tell secrets;" it is equally important that the student does not get these impressions. An invasion of privacy, or even the appearance of the invasion of privacy, can have highly undesirable consequences.

The *school nurse* as a multidisciplinary team member has not been discussed. The nurse is included mainly as a liason person to help provide information of a medical nature and to help mediate the physical examination of the student, when it is indicated. The school nurse should also provide information to the multidisciplinary team on such things as the kind of medication taken by the student, and how the medication might affect the student's behavior. The school nurse can often provide important baseline behavioral information, particularly that related to school "phobic" reactions. The conditions under which an otherwise healthy, happy child reports to the school infirmary often yields important data about the child's history of reinforcement, the interaction between the teacher and the child, and the child's affinity to or aversion for specific classes or courses of study. Recommendation for changes in student-evaluation procedures often come from baselines generated by the school nurse. It is easy to overlook the nurse as a likely source of student characteristics of the highly accessible type. We tend to think of the nurse as providing only the medical and genetic-type data that are sometimes inferential in nature and not highly accessible. More often than not, the nurse can be an important team member in the design of efficient instructional contingencies.

In this section we have discussed the need and the rationale for a multidisciplinary team in the assessment of special education students. We have presented the members of an ideal multidisciplinary team, and a general description of functions and qualifications of the team members. The multidisciplinary team is presented as a method of gathering the necessary data for the placement of most exceptional children, as a method of meeting the requirements of the laws governing the mandatory main-streaming of special children. The focus is clearly on the disabil-ities of the child; in later sections this will not be the case. Eventually the disabilities of the "system" must be confronted, i.e., the various alternatives that must be provided students in terms of instruction, evaluation, and materials and equipment that are not now provided.

After the individual students who are selected by the screening process have been directed through the assessment, after the diagnostic tests have been administered and interpreted (when indicated), after the behavioral and medical data have been collected, what is the next step?

In the traditional setting, this is the point at which a child is ordinarily *placed*. (In the sense that it is used here, "placed" means physical removal to a special, self-contained room). Under main-streaming guidelines, the student is not yet ready for placement, neither in the traditional sense nor by our operational definition. Two very important operations must be interspersed between formal assessment and the "placement" of the program to the student: (1) The development of skills hierarchies (if the system has not already developed them) and (2) discovery of where each of the assessed students happens to be on the skills hierarchies, i.e., how many of the skills has he or she mastered?

In the chapter on placement, it will be seen that many of the options allow for the special students to remain in the "regular" classroom with their age peers. This allowance, while at first appearing to be a rather innocuous requirement, is one which raises a number of serious questions. Among them are: Will there be both group and individual instruction going on in the main-streamed classroom? How will students be evaluated; won't class-room norms be destroyed? Since there will be such a wide discrepancy between students in terms of academic achievement, will it be possible to conduct instruction that will be beneficial to all students? Providing glib "yesses" to these and other questions is easy; showing *how* it is possible to answer "yes" to all of them is the matter that is critical and difficult.

Before mainstreaming can occur, that is before students with widely divergent academic and behavioral characteristics can be taught effectively in a classroom, we must know how to write individual educational programs. We cannot write individual educational programs that fit individual children until we have decided what we would ideally like them to know, and how much of that is already known by them. One of the troublesome problems of traditional education, even with a class population that is said to be "homogeneous," is that some students do not have the necessary academic prerequisites to attack a content area efficiently. Others are already proficient at the content under consideration and must "suffer" through another presentation. The valuable study time of both these groups is wasted in the traditional method of instruction. Whereas the aforementioned is a problem in the traditional classroom in the mainstreamed classroom it shouts for attention. A common-sense beginning to the answer to the problem is the formulation of skills hierarchies. What are skills hierarchies?

Skills hierarchies are specific, behaviorally-stated academic competencies with which to evaluate student academic progress (and, incidentally, to evaluate instructional procedures). Skills hierarchies may also be made up of behaviorally-stated developmental competencies which may be used to get a general idea of how well the student is developed compared to his or her peers. The latter is effective for and appropriate to elementary-aged students. Both academic and developmental skills should be written such that a student can be evaluated with either "can do" or "cannot do." Some examples of *academic* skills are:

Can recognize and pronounce all letters of the alphabet (upper and lower case, manuscript and cursive) without error.

Can solve ten-line, two column addition computation with 90% accuracy.

Some examples of *developmental* skills are:

Can dress him (her) self without assistance.

Can throw a baseball a distance of 10 feet into a two-foot high basket, one foot in diameter, nine times out of 10.

Before implementing a successful mainstreaming program, it is necessary for school systems to actually put skills hierarchies in writing. These competencies should be specified at each grade level and in all disciplines in elementary and middle school. They should be compiled by discipline and by course-name in high schools. Instrumentation should then be devised which will quickly identify those things an individual can and cannot do. Then and only then can individualized instruction proceed *in an efficient manner.*

The first question that comes to mind is, "Won't we be duplicating work; don't most well-sequenced textbooks do that for us?" The answer is "yes" and "no." Yes, the textbooks do list the information and facts in narrative form and suggest either directly and indirectly what one should be able to do after studying the material presented. No, the textbooks do not typically state in behavioral terms, all those things that one *should be able to do,* and state them in the manner prescribed by behavioral approaches to teaching. Additionally, a great quantity of material is presented in the ordinary textbook. Some of the material is directly related to the skills or information the textbooks are intended to impart; other is tangential or is background material which is not absolutely necessary. Still other material is there to make the text more "readable" and is often a part of the author's style of writing. To be more specific, a large amount of information, examples, and stylistic treatments are furnished in most texts, and it is left up to the reader to select the parts that are important, the ways of presenting them, and the methods by which students will demonstrate that they have learned the content. This practice, while allowing the teacher to make an important judgement as to the ability of his or her *class* to learn the material, is one of the main reasons why there is such a skills discrepancy between students in different schools who have used a specific textbook for a course at a particular level. Note that "*class*" is italicized; this is to denote the "group" (as opposed to "individual") nature of the material-selection question. In group or norm-referenced instruction situations the curriculum is selected with the *majority* of the class in mind. Also, each teacher's choice is relatively independent; that is, without rather precise standards for curriculum selection, presentation, and student evaluation, it is reasonable to expect wide variation in content across classes (and schools). For example, if one were to give a comprehensive examination to all students in a given school system who made "B's" in freshman English (the exam being standard and drawn from the same literature text used by all students), the dispersion of scores on the exam would be astounding. Yet their grades ("B") would lead one to believe that they are at the same level of competence in freshman English. By examination of students' performance in relation to a pre-established skills hierarchy it is possible to make a more precise statement of "what a student knows" in relation to "what is desirable to know." Whereas differences in achievement are certain not to be erased by the procedure, the differences that *are* noted with the behavioral evaluation are peculiar to that particular hierarchy. Such procedures make it possible to make an evaluation of: (1) the beginning point for each individual student with regard to a specific list of competencies, (2) "where" each individual student "is" after instruction with regard to that specific list of skills, and hence, (3) the effectiveness of the instruction for each student with regard to the specific list of skills. In plain terms, a "B" in school X would mean precisely the same thing as a "B" in school Y (with regard to specific skills), a condition that would make grades (and diplomas) much more credible and valid as an evaluation device(s). Again, this is not to say that persons receiving instruction and evaluation under such a system would be objectively evaluated in terms of their *complete* fund of knowledge in a given subject or discipline, but that the evaluation would address itself to a restricted and predetermined content—only that listed in the skills hierarchy. Whereas some teachers may be able to evaluate students in a global manner from limited data, such an evaluation would vary in validity from teacher to teacher and virtually guarantee that some students would receive evaluations that are grossly unfair.

The thrust of this section, then, is to point out that there is great value in establishing exactly *what is required* at a particular grade level or course, and discovering exactly how *much of the material is already "known" by each individual student,* both before and after instruction. This allows a student to have an individual program of study. *Individual programs* are highly desirable for homogeneous classes of non-handicapped students, for even in such classes differences in individual ability (endowment) and different histories of reinforcement, coupled with group instruction and evaluation practices have led to wide disparities in student knowledge, discipline by discipline. If individual programs are desirable for homogeneously-grouped students, they are mandatory for heterogeneous classes in which there are both handicapped and non-handicapped students.

How, then, does one go about establishing skills hierarchies? One way is to purchase commercially available lists. Another is to ask each teacher within a system to develop his or her own. The first method, while it allows the teacher to move more quickly into the use of individualized instruction, has a negative effect on the teacher. Most teachers probably feel professionally demeaned and somewhat "dictated to" if they are not allowed some prerogatives of content selection and sequencing. If commercial lists are reused, little or no teacher training occurs; there is always some benefit to be derived from teacher participation in skills-list development. However, if each teacher develops his or her skill hierarchies independently, we are faced with the same outcomes as in the "freshman English" example; namely, the content selected will vary from teacher to teacher. Whereas this would not necessarily remove the objectivity from any other teacher's evaluation of a given child, the curriculum would not be standard across classes and the system. Therefore, a grade of "B" in English I in one class would not be the same as a grade of "B" in another class; neither would evaluations of the type "... objectives

1-24 completed ..." represent the same amount of learning. It also seems to be a waste of human effort and resources to have a large number of people working on the same task, when large numbers of people do not necessarily contribute to the efficiency of the solution. After weighing all possible approaches, most administrators elect to bring together groups of three or four of their "best" teachers in two or three marathon sessions. These groups are selected and given the assignment of stating all the "facts about" and "how to" skills (in behavioral terms) they believe should be learned by students at their grade or department level. These lists are then circulated to the other teachers in the system, with requests for additions and deletions. After all teachers have had a chance to comment on the lists, the initial groups meet again and incorporate the editorial work they feel is appropriate. Each grade level and department level within the system then has a skills list. In the final step, the grade and department levels are compared and the "overlap" is discarded and/or the "gaps" are filled in. This final effort makes it possible to compile a *master list of skills.* Such a list is important for several reasons:

(1) Regardless of a given student's grade level, such a list makes it possible to "know" precisely where the student is on the master list of skills.

(2) Transfer students do not have to flounder helplessly for months, trying to "catch up" with the rest of their class, or be bored to death because the material is "old" to them.

(3) It makes more difficult the "faking" of ignorance when first coming in to a new grade level. For example, when students who are experienced at "faking" move into a new class they begin to protest when new material is introduced. Typically, it happens when the teacher mentions that, "... I assume you are familiar with (for example) the Pythagorian Theorem." The wise student knows that new material can be stalled off with the simple entreaty that "... Mr. Styrofoam didn't cover *that* with us ..." If most of the class maintains that Mr. Styrofoam was, indeed, derelict in his instruc-

tional duties, the teacher feels forced to give in, and consequently wastes valuable instruction time covering old material. With a master list of specified skills, and with a student record that has been maintained and is up-to-date, students cannot get by with "faking it."

(4) Perhaps the most important reasons for skills hierarchies is that they allow the student to move forward in the academic material at his or her own pace. Not only does it relieve the boredom that is present in a student who is in a norm-referenced instructional system and happens to be above the norm, but is a key consideration in removing undue stress from students who are behind the norm.

(5) Skills hierarchies allow the teacher to employ principles of operant theory more effectively. With specifically stated skills to be learned and which are presented to the student in a fashion that does not induce boredom and stress, it is highly likely that learning can be almost entirely rewarding; at least it allows the discontinuation of punishment of academic behaviors. Many teachers do not stop to think about their actions, and if they did, they would be the strongest advocates of skills hierarchies. One could take the example of any student who is significantly away from the norm in achievement in a class that is taught and evaluated in a norm-referenced fashion. It is highly likely that most of the academic behaviors emitted by such a student are going to be met with punishing consequences. Operant theory teaches us that most of our behavior is operant; that is, it is shaped, maintained, and/or extinguished by the consequences it receives. Behavior that is constantly punished, or simply not rewarded, will eventually extinguish. Not only that, negative feelings which typically accompany punishment or non-reward become attached to the behaviors to which they give rise. Therefore, it seems mandatory to arrange conditions so that as often as possible, *academic effort* will be rewarded. The absence of skills hierarchies make it difficult to do so, and for the reasons enumerated so far.

(6) Skills hierarchies remove the "guess-work" for the student. For example, in a norm-referenced instructional situation, teacher X gives a reading assignment covering A, B, and C materials. The teacher reveals that there will be an important test over the materials, and that the test will count for half of the students' final grades for that semester. Test-wise students begin to ask questions. "What kind of a test is it; will it be objective-type or essay? How many items will there be? *Can you give us some idea of what we should learn?*" Teachers will sometimes give a direct and correct answer to the first two questions; it is rare when the third question is answered directly and correctly. This kind of evasiveness communicates quite clearly to the student that the teacher's object is *not* for the student to perform well on the test, but rather, it seems to the student that the teacher is trying to outsmart him. The student is faced with three alternatives, all of which are non-productive and anxiety-arousing: One can elect to attempt to learn *every* detail in the reading assignment—and in most cases this is next to impossible. One can try to second-guess the teacher as to what items will be on the test. Some teachers are highly predictable; others are not. A third alternative is to say "... to hell with it ..." Skills hierarchies remove the kind of guess-work just described.

In summary, skills hierarchies are necessary to the establishment of individual instructional programs. Individual programs cannot be effectively written or implemented without knowing specifically what is to be learned, and how much of that material the student already knows. Skills hierarchies must be established: they may come from commercial sources, from individual teachers working independently, or from small groups of "master" teachers, with editorial work being shared by the teachers' professional peers on common grade or department levels. Skills hierarchies are not sufficiently spelled out in text books, as some teachers believe. The use of skills hierarchies make the grading process or system more relevant to the academic competencies it purports to evaluate. Skills hierarchies prevent student "faking" and teacher "trickery." They allow for individual student-learning speed-differences and promote the effective use of operant theory by the teacher.

Postscript to Screening, Assessment, and Placement

Since the entire procedure of screening, assessment, and placement is more than a little complex and somewhat different from traditional procedures, it is perhaps worthwhile to review the entire process.

The screening process begins by a systematic review of all students in a given class, school or system. The students are all compared to standard criteria such as performance on standardized measures of achievement (group tests), standardized symptom checklists, standard lists of chronic medical conditions, and subjective impressions of teachers; mainly having to do with interpersonal behaviors in the classroom. With the exception of the last index, standard cut-off levels are used to select those students who are recommended for the formal assessment procedure.

Once these students are identified, parents or guardians of the children are notified of the decision, given the criteria by which their child(ren) were selected, and asked to agree to the formal assessment. In the event the parent disagrees, the child is placed in the group of "regular" students and the matter is not pursued any further. In certain extreme cases where the parents disagree and the student would suffer appreciably (in the opinion of the consulting or referring teacher), an effort is made by school officials to get the parent to reconsider and allow the assessment to take place. This is usually initiated by and arranged for by the school principal. If this effort fails, a record is kept of the efforts, and the child is placed in the "regular" program. Those children who are approved for formal assessment are directed to the assessment process.

The multidisciplinary team receives the screening data collected on each child to be assessed. A "profile" is constructed in which the team can look at academic information, symptom data, and the referring teacher's impressions on the child's interpersonal behavior, along with the medical information. A standard questionnaire which asks for information concerning interests, hobbies, general areas of academic strengths, weaknesses and preferences, a brief medical history including current medication being taken by the child, sleeping habits, and any "open-ended" type of data the parents may feel is important in devising the child's educational program is furnished the parent. The child is interviewed (if the age and intellectual condition of the child so indicates) asking for essentially the same information, including the request for the name of a person or persons who might serve as an ad hoc member of the multidisciplinary team. The parent's questionnaire also makes a request for candidates to serve as ad hoc members on the child's multidisciplinary team. The referring teacher or principal may also have names of persons they would like to see serve on the child's multidisciplinary team. The multidisciplinary team itself will make the final decision on who shall serve as the ad hoc member. When the questionnaire is received back from the parent and the multidisciplinary team selects the ad hoc member, the profile of the child is completed and a conference is scheduled. The parent and the ad hoc member are not invited to the conference unless the team feels that a program cannot be written without their "input."

The conference discusses the information that might indicate that an outside evaluation (medical, psychiatric, etc.) is indicated. If so, the child is referred to the school system's central-office pupil-personnel service staff with recommendations on the outside evaluation. The recommendation should include the professional(s) who should conduct the evaluation, what kind of data are expected, and should specify the contingencies that are possible. For instance, the referral may be to confirm a particular chronic medical condition, and to obtain a professional opinion as to why the child should or should not be allowed to attend regular classes on campus. The central-office organization should carry out the evaluation (or see that it is done) and send the information back to the multidisciplinary team.

If an outside evaluation should not be in order, the multi-disciplinary team should proceed directly to find exactly where the student is academically. This is done by using the academic and developmental skills hierarchies to determine at which skills the child is accomplished and at which skills he or she is deficient or does not have. Once this is accomplished, it is the team's responsibility to make a determination (tentative in nature) as to whether the skills listed as ideal by the school are appropriate for the child. There may be endowment, background, or current environmental-conditions that suggest that certain of the established skills are not appropriate for the child to pursue. There may be some skills that *are* appropriate for the child to pursue, but which do not appear on the skills hierarchies. In any event, the child's program should be formulated with the preceding considerations in mind, avoiding inclusion of these skills at which the student is already proficient, and including only those at which the student is not proficient but which are recommended for him or her. The program should take the form of instructional objectives. The objectives must contain measurable behaviors and the minimum level of acceptable performance predetermined and stated in the objectives. Each objective must be accompanied by a specific list of materials, equipment and/or lecture content that are geared to the achievement of each objective. Each objective must be matched with a description of both teacher and student activities. The activities must be logically related to the goals of the objectives. The multidisciplinary team must make the decision as to approximately how long the achievement of the objectives will take, and enough objectives must be prepared or listed in the child's program to comprise at least *one* academic grading-period. If possible, the child's program should extend over a longer period, but the multidisciplinary team must, at the termination of no more than one academic grading-period subsequent to the preparation of the program, review the child's accomplishments of the objectives and make the necessary adjustments indicated in terms of type and amount of content, structure of the objectives, materials, equipment, and activities. The child must also be reviewed at the end of each grading period for possible change in program option. Each child's academic evaluation shall consist of an individual listing of the entire program that has been set forth for that grading period, and shall be marked, objective by objective, as to "complete" or "incomplete." The parent shall be furnished with a copy of the evaluation, and shall be granted an explanatory interview with one or more members of the multidisciplinary team if it is so requested. In no instance should a special child be evaluated with and "A," "B," "C," etc., letter grade. The child's accomplishments must stand as the evaluation.

In instances of outside evaluation which results in *either* an inside or an outside placement, the child's program shall be prepared in the same manner as described above, and shall be subject to the same contingencies listed above.

It must be kept in mind that at any point in any child's program, the parent may invoke "due process." The due-process procedures are listed elsewhere in this section, and are not subject to arbitrary revision or change by any educational personnel or official.

Chapter **4**

Traditional Referral and Assessment, Versus the Mainstream Approach

IN THIS CHAPTER we will be presenting the referral and placement process from two points of view. We will first describe the traditional referral and placement process in detail, pointing out the individuals involved and the options of each individual. Special emphasis will be placed on the role of the teacher. After summing up the traditional process, we will describe the new multilevel approach mandated by states' laws across 48 of the 50 states. Finally, we will compare and contrast the two techniques.

The traditional format followed in diagnosing and placing a child in a special education program has varied from system to system and, indeed, from school to school. There are several common features involved in the traditional procedures, however, that can be cited as representative of past placement techniques. Generally, the child is identified as something other than "normal" by the classroom teacher based on either behavioral or performance anomalies. If the problem is not "severe" (if the teacher can put up with the behavior in the classroom) little if anything is done. Anecdotal records and word of mouth communication generally spread the word that "this child is different," or "this child is bad." Very often the "diagnostic" process stops here. The child, whatever his problem, is identified by the classroom teacher and the word is spread to other individuals in an informal fashion. Children with problems are apt to spend several years languishing in normal programs without the aid necessary for the maximization of their individual development.

All this seems rather incredulous, but an examination of "teacher diagnosis" before outlining the remainder of the traditional format should serve to shed some light on the matter. To facilitate this process we will examine teacher training and capabilities, the attitudes traditionally encouraged among teachers, and the effects of striving for mediocrity.

Teacher training (as has been and will be emphasized throughout this book) is an incredibly important factor in the diagnosis and placement of children. As of the time of this writing, students enrolled in traditional elementary or secondary education programs are not required to take any courses dealing with the identification and correction of disabilities that children who are eligible for special educational services may possess. In other words, the teacher in the "normal" classroom receives no formal training in the identification of children with educational problems. The theory seems to be that such teachers should "intuit" problems and somehow refer the student to the "proper authorities" for diagnosis (remember, teachers teach, counselors counsel, school psychologists psychologize, and the poor special education teachers take the children off everyone's hands). Unfortunately, most schools are characterized by a "don't-rock-the-boat" attitude that filters down to include all the faculty. Referring a child because a teacher suspects something is wrong is boat-rocking behavior. Just because Billy seems a little slow, or because Joe acts strangely from time to time is no "real" reason to disturb the counselor or psychologist. The teacher could easily be wrong and wouldn't these people be angry if the child was really normal? What will (gasp!) the parents say if the child is referred? No one wants to endure the wrath of angry and upset parents. What will be the final impact on me, the teacher? I might be transferred to Slumgullion High. It's probably better to put up with Joe's behavior and coax Billy a little harder than to disturb all these people and risk recrimination. Besides, with no formal training or practice in diagnosis, it is so easy to be wrong.

Luckily, not all teachers are milquetoasts or are afraid to rock the boat. If they were, children would never be referred to other sources. Referral has tended to occur only when the problems were so severe as to drastically damage the teacher's self-perceived classroom effectiveness; when children are so obviously alienated by other children as to necessitate change as a matter of survival for the child; or when the children are obviously not achieving at anything close to an acceptable rate of intellectual development. "Minor" problems, of course, are the province of the teacher and woe unto the teacher who holds the best interests of each child at heart and tries to make referrals when calamity is not imminent. In effect, the teacher of normal children has not been given the professional leverage, through training, informal power structures, and ambiguity of responsibility to allow for adequate referral service.

There are many other gaps we see in current teacher education programs besides the obvious one in the identification and treatment of educational problems. These shortcomings and the remedies for these shortcomings will be thoroughly discussed in Chapter 7.

Lack of appropriate training, and hence, lack of teacher capability in diagnosis is not the only problem in the traditional approach to referral. The *general attitude* of most schools, as we pointed out previously, is one of protecting the status quo. Each individual is slotted into his or her informal position in the school hierarchy based on the perceived power and responsibilities of the various jobs held throughout the school. "Teachers just do not diagnose. Why, we have a county-wide psychologist who pulls down a big salary that does all our diagnosing." Taken a little further is the relationship that has existed between the administrations of many schools and the teacher. "The teacher may come to me with his or her problem, but I, as the principal, will decide if the problem is really important." Are you getting the drift of what we are saying here? What we mean is that the stereotype of jobs in schools has determined for us the state of referrals in schools. Everyone fits in their nice little slot and everybody knows what his or her responsibilities are and they had better not step out of line—or else.

The third major contributing factor to the difficulty in referrals has been the active *striving in American education for mediocrity*. You see, the majority of teachers are trained to teach at some hypothetical mean, an invisible average of ability, an unknown average child. They are taught to teach at the level of the "average student." Translated into working terms this means that most kids will make "C's" (60%), there will be a few "D's" and "B's" (13 or 14% of each) and very few "A's" and "F's" (6% of each). Obviously this results in most students doing passing work with some very good marks and some that are very bad. The teacher is taught to accept as appropriate the facts that this teaching-for-the-mean will result in several bored children that have never been challenged or fulfilled by the course content. There is always going to be a certain percentage of children that make "A's." They don't have to work hard. It's normal. For these children school becomes a place of boredom, a place that offers no challenge to thoughts or abilities, a place that wastes the time and ability of the gifted child. Don't worry, though, it's very common, very predictable.

On the other side of the coin, teachers are taught that a certain percentage of children will never do well in school. This, too, is acceptable and highly predictable. There will always be frustrated, angry, shame-filled or defiant children that will fail, in school and ultimately in life. This is acceptable, though the average student does average work and these children are just below average. School for these children can become a source of pain, shame, guilt, embarrassment, and hate. The abilities and lives of these children are of little consequence, though. After all, it is all very predictable.

This acceptance of boredom and unfulfilledness on the one hand and hostility and failure on the other is the direct result of the teaching philosophies of the past several years and leads to the easy tolerance, acceptance, and almost encouragement given to retaining the status quo. "So what if Billy has failed every test this year and doesn't seem to understand any of the material. After all, a certain percentage of the children *have* to fail, you know. And of course he's going to be angry, but he'll just have to 'buckle down' and really become motivated before he can pass." Statements like this are an indictment of our entire educational process. The acceptance of failure as a normal occurrence does more to frustrate proper referral and placement than any other factor.

When the traditional gets going

When the child finally reaches the referral process, his problems are by no means over. The referral process is similar to any red-tape-filled bureaucratic program and involves a series of inter-relating offices with the decisions for action made at each level. Communication, not surprisingly, is minimal. For an example of a very simple referral and placement service, let us follow one student through the ordeal.

When entering the referral process the student may originally be referred to the principal, the vice-principal or this person's equivalent, or perhaps the guidance counselor. We will examine the process taking each person involved in turn and describe the cptions open to them and the possible result of each option.

(A) The principal.

If the child is referred to the principal by the teacher, four options appear to be available. The first option the principal has, as chief administrator of the school, is to "discipline" (punish) the child. The second option is to counsel the child and the third option is to refer the child to another individual. The fourth option is to involve the parents, either by inviting them to participate or by visiting the home and getting to the "bottom" of the matter. Looking at these options in turn, we see that the first option, punishment, is appropriate only if the child has no real emotional problem, i.e., the child has merely misbehaved in "normal" fashion and the teacher has felt that the "big gun" should be called in to emphasize the seriousness of the misbehavior. If the child is disturbed, if he suffers from a "real" mental disturbance, a real pathology, then the first option is futile and will provide no positive results. The second option, counseling the child, as well as the fourth option, visiting the home, are generally not viable options considering the common presence of better qualified staff members to perform this function. The training and inclination of most chief administrators precludes the counseling visitation process. The third option, referral to another person, seems to be the best option as the principal, although eminently qualified in many areas, is not a likely source of placement or problem resolution for the child.

(B) The hatchet person.

In large schools, the immediate referral for problem children is the vice-principal (vice-principals, discipline teachers, and coaches all serve as hatchet people for misbehaviors from time to time). The vice-principal has options identical to those of the principal with the addition of referring the child back to the principal. The outcomes can be considered to be nearly the same when we take into account that many vice-principals are less well trained than the principal. Irrespective of the student's level of distress, if pathology is involved, referral to either the principal or vice-principal can be effective only if further referral is the option they choose. In practical terms the involvement of the principal or vice-principal results only in an extra step in the referral program.

(C) The counselor.

The next person along the referral trail that our child may see is the guidance counselor. The options open to the guidance counselor are more varied than previous ones we have investigated and should be more hopeful. The guidance counselor may opt to: (1) engage the student in personal counseling; (2) engage the student in group counseling; (3) administer *some* personality assessment instruments and work for a solution from the results; (4) investigate home and classroom environments and initiate change; and (5) refer the child again. The competent guidance counselor will probably try several of the options available. Decisions as to further referral should be based on a firm diagnosis of the child grounded on knowledge gained from the first four options. If changes brought about by options one to four are significant, the referral process may stop here with the child returning to the classroom while the counselor continues to help the child work out his or her problems. Unfortunately, most guidance counselors are responsible for 200 to 1000 students and they may not have the time or inclination to engage in a full helping relationship. If this is the case, or if the child is found to be more severely disturbed than the counselor can manage (or, incidentally, if the counselor as is sometimes the case, is incompetent due to personality or training variables), the child will again be referred. (There is the problem here, too, of a child's problem falling beyond the scope of a counselor's abilities and yet remaining in the care of the counselor rather than being referred to a more appropriate person. This is not a widespread phenomenon, but it does happen more often than we would like.)

(D) The physician.

Occasionally certain individuals in the referral process may suspect organic damage as the basis of the child's problem. If this is the case for any number of organic problems, e.g., vision, hearing, nutrition, brain damage, etc., the child is generally referred to a medical doctor for diagnosis. Most large school systems have doctors retained for such services while many smaller systems must rely on private physicians contacted through the parents. In any case, the doctor's options are limited to diagnosis, treatment, or referral to a specialist. If the treatment is successful, then the child may continue in the regular classroom. If the prognosis is less optimistic, or if further referral is indicated, the child moves one step further in his or her ordeal. (The visit to the doctor may or may not be included and is cited here as one commonly occurring part of the whole referral process.)

(E) The social worker.

Occasionally a social worker may be involved if the school system is large enough. They are usually involved if the problem is believed to stem from problems in the home. Social workers vary from individual to individual in terms of their success. The social worker tends not to diagnose as much as treat suspected problems. If the social worker finds the problem to be beyond the scope of his or her abilities, the child is generally referred once more. The social worker has the options of (1) dealing with the problem directly, (2) referring the child, or (3) initiating legal action. If the social worker is successful in dealing with the problem in the home or if further referral is deemed necessary, the child moves on again.

(F) The school psychologist.

The last step in the diagnosis process is usually the school psychologist. This individual, (if, indeed, such an individual is available which is not often the case) generally administers an exhaustive battery of tests to the student and on the basis of these results and previous reports, refers the child to the terminal goal in the process. The terminal goal consists of a return to the classroom with some ongoing treatment, placement in a special education class for children with similar problems, or institutionalization. The result of these options in the majority of cases is to get the child out of the hair of the classroom teacher and locked into a "special program" so that he or she won't bother anyone any more.

As you may have gathered, this process is a highly time consuming one, often taking more than two years to complete. Although our hypothetical student was emotionally disturbed, the process is nearly identical for other forms of educational problems. Further, in the traditional process, parents may or may not be kept informed, and at any rate, they have extremely limited input; usually directly proportional to their income and status in the community.

Each individual in the referral process must also re-evaluate the child, passing along his or her recommendations and information to the next person. Often this form of communication is very poor (have you ever glanced through a child's cumulative folder and read the teachers' comments from five years before?). This lack of communication insures the replication of efforts to the same end over and over. At best the traditional process is cumbersome, confusing, secretive, frustrating, time consuming, and culminates in questionable results. Perhaps the most significant shortcoming of the traditional form of referral and placement is the lack of *educational* diagnosis and placement. The referrals in the traditional format are invariably completed by the etiology of the problem, i.e., the problem is diagnosed (the term labeled is much more appropriate as the "diagnosis" seems to translate to: find the name for the problem) and the child is grouped with other children sharing this diagnosis and is, hence, rooted out of the normal classroom. Nowhere in the process is any provision made for the development of an educational program for the child. It is assumed that if the child is labeled appropriately and sent to an isolated classroom full of similarly labeled children, he or she will somehow profit from the experience. The emphasis of the entire referral and placement process, in fact, has been on eliminating the child as a problem rather than on helping the child.

Attitudes and ambiguity

The traditional referral and placement process, in and of itself, has enough problems to merit its replacement with a more streamlined and less bureaucratic successor. The problems inherent in the "nook" principle (often referred to by the authors as the "schnook" principle), however, further worsen the entire process. The nook principle is that principle that people in ambiguously defined positions seem to operate by. There are certain guidelines to follow if adherence to the nook principle is to be insured: (1) when in trouble or in doubt, run in circles, scream and shout; (2) never make a decision if it can be passed along to someone else; (3) never commit yourself; (4) memorize and immediately recall and repeat as necessary the phrases "it's not our policy" and/or "it's a gut-level feeling"; (5) always keep your own best interest at heart; lastly, (6) above all, keep other people on their toes by demonstrating that you indeed have some power by exercising capricious whims from time to time. This nook principle is not wholly facetious. Due to the nature of the ambiguity of many positions in education we seem to actively encourage poor administrative functioning. This lack of administrative ability does very little to help along students going through the referral and placement process. Indeed, they often become pawns to be struggled over by players of the game seeking to determine who has which power.

Even when the nook (schnook) principle is not in operation, unfortunate attitudes tend to prevail during the referral process. Children in need of referral and placement are often thought of as "problem children." Rather than having the personnel along the referral route deal with them as "people," the children in need of referral are dealt with as "problems," something closely akin to a mechanical malfunction that must be corrected or eliminated. This attitude reduces children to some irritating stimulus to be eliminated. A dehumanizing process, indeed.

New Programs for Screening, Assessment, and Placement

The new multilevel assessment process is designed to remediate the abuses of referral and placement that have become part of the traditional programs. As with any new program, success cannot be guaranteed. Evaluation of the new assessment process must wait until it has been functioning for a considerable amount of time.

The guidelines provided at this time for the multilevel assessment process are general in nature, allowing for flexibility in implementation. They are designed, however, to maximize the effectiveness of each individual in the process.

A side step at this point is perhaps appropriate. Educators at all levels give lip service to the undeniable rights of each child under their tutelage. The problem crops up in the implementations of this process. Rhetoric concerning rights of students and the action of people in ensuring these rights are two very different propositions. In a school system in which a psychologist must serve several thousand students, the sheer mass of work often reduces the involvement with each child to that of the most expedient possible choice. This has been the outcome of the traditional referral and placement process, not only for psychologists, but for all the school personnel. There is no doubt that with current staffing and with the economic slowdown, the new programs will be just as susceptible to decisions based on expediency rather than on the best interests of the students.

The process we describe is not a cure-all or an academic panacea. It is, however, a step in the right direction. Changes in staffing and funding may be necessary to fully carry out the new process, but the best must be done with what is available.

The first step in developing educational programs that will insure that each child has an appropriate educational opportunity is to identify the children among the larger population that require supplemental services. In each of the new state laws enacted recently, the local school systems have the responsibility of developing and initiating a program of screening and assessment within the school system. In most states this is accomplished with the aid of the state government and its resources. This part of the chapter will describe the necessary components of new programs that have been or must be developed to meet the new guidelines.

Assessment has and does refer to the gathering of relevant information that can contribute to accurate and meaningful decisions concerning the educational future of children. The traditional method, as we pointed out above, has not adequately provided this necessary service. There has historically been very little, if any, relationship between diagnosing a child's problem and the formulation of academic planning for the child. Mental retardation has been a psychometric diagnosis, built around the performance of a child on batteries of "intelligence tests." Emotional disturbance has been a psychological or psychiatric diagnosis based on personality tests and interviews. Neurological malfunctions have been medically diagnosed. The diagnosis and placement in these cases, however, have very seldom led to any form of educational strategies to be implemented for the child.

Assessment should not be conducted solely in the contrived settings of artificial testing and interviewing situations. The misunderstandings, secrecy and arbitrariness of traditional data gathering must be altered to alleviate these problems by affording the right to both the parents and the child to be included in the assessment process and the right to fully informed consent.

To meet the new multi-level guidelines for assessment and evaluation six general components must be included in the process. The states' guidelines emphasize the clear indication of inclusion and compliance with these components by the local school systems in order to demonstrate the adoption of state level criteria. These areas of emphasis may be slightly different semantically from state to state but they are highly similar in terms of the process they identify:

1. Primary prevention

2. Multidisciplinary assessment

3. Multifaceted assessment

4. Behavioral-oriented assessment

5. Naturalistic assessment

6. Continuous evaluation

Primary prevention.

As with any useful program, prevention of future problems is highly important. The emphasis of most of the states' programs is placed on prevention as the first priority. The earlier in a child's educational program that potential academic difficulties can be identified, the less costly and more effective programs will be that are designed to overcome the problems. The major emphasis of any assessment program should be aimed at the identification of preschool and kindergarten children that have conditions that may cause disruption or difficulty in school during later years. These children should be screened medically (e.g., physical difficulties in vision, hearing, motor control, brain damage, and other structural impairments), psychometrically (e.g., determination of self-concept, emotional stability, familial intra-relationships, peer relationships, and evidence of any pathology), and intellectually.

Identification at the earliest stages of educational development will allow for the development of less costly and more effective special educational programming. Further, the social and psychological difficulties involved in late identification (e.g., rejection, shame, guilt, hate, feelings of failure, and fear) will be greatly attenuated if not eliminated all together. If special programs can be put into effect on or before entrance into the first grade, it is much more likely that behavioral, social, and emotional problems will be avoided as well as maximizing the students' learning potentials. Feelings of failure and lack of self-worth will be diminished in earlier identification, ensuring the treatment of each individual as a separate, special, human being with the worth of every other individual, and not as slow, lazy, different, bad or stupid.

Multidisciplinary assessment

The new guidelines promote multidisciplinary assessment. The general agreement across states now is that no one professional has the prerogative or the right to restrict assessment to themselves (indeed, or to have it restricted to them by supervisors or other school personnel). In fact, assessment should not be limited to those groups designated as professionals when other school/community members have input that they, the child, or parents feel is of value.

Since behavior can easily be demonstrated to be situation-specific, i.e., there need be little consistency in behavior across varying environments, multidisciplinary assessment is an important component of the new multi-level assessment process. The multidisciplinary assessment procedure must include special-education specialists (generally this position is filled by the school psychologist, the guidance counselor, the social worker, a special education teacher, or the consulting teacher), the child's regular classroom teachers (this means all of them, not just the referrer), and the child's parents or guardians. On most occasions the principal, or a person acting in his place, must be present to represent the top-level administration of the school. This is the minimum number of people that must be prepared to participate in the decision-making meeting. Ideally, any number of people (the bus driver, a cafeteria worker, a teacher aide, or any other concerned person) may sit in on the decision meeting in order to provide pertinent input during the meeting.

The parents' role as an integral part of the evaluation process is to provide background information about the child and to ensure the correct interpretation of the child's behavior. (Note: The inclusion of the parents cannot be restricted to those cases in which the parents are well educated or well informed. The school personnel must ensure that all parents, even if some are not literate, have as full an understanding of the process involved as possible. The emphasis is on the human rights of every child and every parent, regardless of the level of income, education, or social standing of the parents. Whatever time and methods are necessary to ensure parent understanding will be carried out. Under no circumstances will parents be left out because "they wouldn't understand." It is the school personnel's responsibility to see that they do understand.)

In this manner, viable educational programs will be chosen for the child by the group involved. Diagnosis and placement is no longer enough. Decisions as to the actual educational format to be followed by the child must be made. The final implementation of the decision, of course, rests with the principal, the highest-ranking administration officer present at the meeting (or represented at the meeting, as the case may be).

At this point we feel the need to digress momentarily. We have come in contact with literally hundreds of teachers and other personnel that will be affected by the laws and on many occasions have noticed a particular attitude concerning the multidisciplinary approach that needs to be rectified in some manner by the individuals in question. Some of the personnel view the inclusion of all parents in the assessment process with disdain at best, or with open hostility at worst. Comments such as "they're not trained in the area;" "we are professionally trained and they are not;" and "how can you expect some of 'those people' to understand anything? They'll just interfere and ruin the whole process." This attitude of skepticism, contempt, and mistrust must be alleviated. In practical terms people with such attitudes have no real choice, the law specifies what is to be done. The transition to the new process, however, can be impeded and imperiled if such attitudes (and actions to carry out the attitudes) are not changed. No one, teachers and other school personnel included, like to be dictated to, but the change in our assessment programs are necessary to ensure the rights of each and every child, maximizing their collective educational futures.

Multifaceted assessment.

Unfortunately, assessment programs in American schools tend to rely too heavily on standardized test instruments. This has resulted in evaluations based solely on test-score results and not on the children's performance in real-life situations. The American culture is so varied from area to area and from ethnic group to ethnic group that the term standardized loses its value when applied to the wide variety of students that are evaluated by instruments with questionable normative groups. This kind of single source evaluation will no longer be considered acceptable as the means for evaluating any child's condition. This is not to say that the standardized instruments are not helpful, they are. Results of such tests should, however, be interpreted with care and with the special attention to the normative groups. The results, further, should not be generalized past the intent of the test, i.e., an I.Q. test should only be related to whatever definition of intelligence the test indicates (if indeed such definitions have any meaning at all). It should also be kept in mind that any standardized test will have a rather high variance level, one standard deviation (usually ±10 points on an I.Q. test to ±20 points). This variance must be considered when interpreting any standardized instrument. (Incidentally, most of the interpretive manuals that accompany the tests provide information concerning this variance and caution about the test-retest reliability, i.e., the fact that the same student taking the same test on different occasions may make quite different scores.)

To meet the requirements for multifaceted assessment it will be necessary to gather information from real-life and classroom situations. Because of this requirement, assessment should include direct observation of the child in a wide variety of possible settings. These observations must be made with concrete terminology and specific behaviors in mind and not become generalizations. For example, merely stating that a child mis-behaves says very little. However, specific referral to specified behavior such as hitting others, sleeping in class, etc., allow for meaningful communication. (Note: Simple as communication concerning student behavior may seem, there is a great deal of ambiguity if the behaviors are not properly specified. When we say a student is not attentive, what do we mean? Do we mean that the child is looking out the window? Is the child sleeping? Is the child merely not giving signs of recognition of the class material? Do we mean all these things? As you can see, even so simple a term as non-attentiveness can become quite ambiguous when we keep in mind that many people must interpret whatever terms we use. A better example may be the problem of a child not appreciating the class. Ah! What could we mean by appreciate? Does appreciate mean to do all the homework? Does it mean to make above "90" on all the tests? Does it mean to do extra work outside the class? Appreciate probably means all these things and more to any large group of people. The authors recall one English professor who measured what he called appreciation of literature from students' results on unbelievably exacting, total-recall discussion tests.

Interviews with people that are important factors in the child's life are also necessary. These interviews furnish data from a wide variety of situations and from a wide field of personal interpre-tations. Classwork, including homework, in-class projects, teacher-prepared tests, workbooks, and other materials, must also be included in the evaluation as well as standardized test-instruments, the interview data, and data from direct observation.

Assessment of classroom behavior should fall into two categories as delineated by Williams and Anadam (1973). These two forms of assessment are product and process assessment. *Product assessment* is the evaluation of the child's products in comparison with the products of other children. That is, such products as papers, art work, teacher-made test results, and special projects are evaluated to determine the child's level of functioning. More accurately, the child's level of functioning is inferred from the product. Product assessment refers not only to academic behavior but also to social behavior, where products such as social isolation or rejection are possible.

Product assessment, however, is only a portion of the multifaceted assessment process. *Process assessment,* the assessment of the process (those behaviors from start to finish that culminate in a final product, e.g., all the behaviors that lead up to the taking of a teacher-made test) leading up to a product is a necessary complement to the product assessment. Process assessment (which we will explore more thoroughly in the instruction chapter) allows examination of each of the steps involved in developing any product and in this manner permits a determination of what, exactly, causes the product to result as it is.

This wide-scope program of evaluation, including a wide variety of sources, should provide more pertinent information on which more appropriate diagnoses can be made as when compared to the restriction of evaluation to standardized instruments.

Behaviorally-oriented assessment

Behaviorally-oriented assessment refers to the use of procedures that provide for the evaluation of non-ambiguous concepts. Emphasis is placed on observable, measurable and replicable behavior, not on terms such as "retarded," "mentally deficient," "agressive," "hyperactive," and the like.

Terms (labels) such as "disoriented," "emotionally disturbed," "mentally ill," "educably retarded," and similar labels for broad classes of behaviors cannot be measured or interpreted without extensive definitions. They are, at best, ambiguous labels that can be differently interpreted by each person that uses the term. Identifying a child, for instance, as "emotionally disturbed," does very little to identify the behaviors that have culminated in the label "emotionally disturbed." Merely interpreting or summarizing a series of behaviors with some label is no longer acceptable. Assessment must deal with the levels of specific, concrete, and discrete behaviors that lead to the diagnosis. These, as previously mentioned, must be reported in measurable and observable form, e.g., hitting another child, screaming, hitting head, pulling hair, etc. This form of assessment does away with the often arbitrary judgements of behavior and emphasizes the actual behaviors in a form that attenuates subjective levels within the judgement process.

Naturalistic assessment

Naturalistic assessment is exactly what the term implies. It requires that data be carried out in settings outside of the artificial constraints of the psychologist's office. The data should be accumulated in places where the child lives, e.g., his home, neighborhood, playground, or church; and in places where the child works, e.g., the classroom. Such assessment requires viewing the behavior (in person) in real-life situations. Naturalistic assessment is a direct, primary assessment conducted at those places where the behavior occurs naturally. Higher validity is expected in judgements made about future educational programming when the child is viewed as he actually performs the behavior in the classroom, home, or neighborhood, than if levels of behavior inferred from indirect sources are relied upon as has often been the case.

The interaction of the child with those persons that are important figures in his life (e.g., parents, teachers, peers, and siblings) is included in such data gathering procedures and provides pertinent data for the evaluation of the "whole" child. Further, specific stimuli (people, places, or things) that evoke certain behaviors can be determined, a result that cannot be accomplished in traditional forms of assessment.

The constraints of artificial environments such as psychologists', counselors', or principals' offices are such that behavioral assessment is likely to have little validity when compared to naturalistic assessment. The purpose of this component of the assessment program, naturalistic assessment, is to provide the most valid, reliable and pertinent data possible to the over-all evaluation process. Inferring from an office call or from a set of test results is one thing, but the actual observance of behavior in the natural environment is something else, totally. It is the only way in which the fairest possible assessment of each individual can be made.

Assessment in contrived settings.

Situation specificity refers to a phenomenon common to all organisms. Quite simply, organisms (people included) behave differently in different situations. We are all familiar with the example of Mr. Smith's rowdy and unruly class moving across the hall at the beginning of the new period and behaving like little angels in Miss Bludgeon's class. We all behave differently in different environments. We certainly would not use some of the language we use on the golf course or in a bowling alley in church. Children, of course, are no exception to this phenomenon. A child may misbehave very seriously in the classroom and behave like a "perfect" child in the office. Of course, children may also behave quite differently from classroom to classroom.

Continuous evaluation.

To be effective, assessment must be an ongoing, continuous process. The teacher, parents and other important people involved in the child's educational program must have continuous feedback in order to alter and tailor educational programs for the maximum benefit of the students. Constant evaluation removes the time between the identification of the student's problem or impedance and the actions that follow to attenuate the problem. The assessment program for any child experiencing learning difficulties cannot be a one-shot attempt with follow-ups every few years. The states encourage and demand constant measurement and evaluation of the child's functioning. Indeed, if we, as educators are to properly serve our students, we must be constantly measuring and evaluating our teaching techniques and our students' progress. We must constantly change in order to meet their needs. After all, that's what we're in business for.

The traditional and the new, multi-level programs compared.

No doubt, by this point in the chapter the reader has already made several comparisons and contrasts between traditional assessment procedures and the new, multi-level approach. To facilitate this process we will take one student through the multi-level assessment process and compare this procedure to the one we described in the first section of this chapter.

The major emphasis, of course, in multi-level assessment is on early identification and prevention, something that has not been emphasized previously. To make our example more lucid, however, we will assume that the identification process for our hypothetical student will start with her in the eighth grade. With the inclusion, now, of continuous assessment our hypothetical child is rapidly identified by her work in the classroom which is not up to acceptable levels for a child of her age. She is no longer accepted or tolerated as "one of those who must inevitably fail" and the total assessment program begins. Similar to the traditional process, she is referred to the school psychologist for a battery of tests and interview appraisals. However, in our multi-level referral and placement process, the psychologist and teachers are now observing the child in the natural environment with emphasis on behavioral assessment, not labeling. Data is gathered from several sources and the parents are informed as to the initiation of the process and are kept posted on the progress. After a relatively short period of time (this varies from state to state but generally is about three weeks) the assessment team (psychologist, counselor, teachers, principal, parents, child and other concerned people) meet to assess the total scope of the child and make educational prescriptions for the child. The parents are kept fully informed and have a hand in the decision making process. The decision is no longer one of finding the correct label for the child, but is now a matter of determining the correct educational future for the child. After the decision has been made, with the fully informed consent of the parents, the assessment procedure does not stop but is constant as long as the child remains in school.

The advantages of multi-level assessment over traditional assessment are as follows:

1. Full informed consent by parents

2. Evaluation is constant

3. Follow up is constant

4. Assessment occurs in natural conditions

5. All interested persons are included in the process

6. Decisions are made by the total group and not by one individual (implementation and closure is the responsibility of the principal)

7. Data is gathered in many different ways

8. Educational decisions are made, not pathological ones

9. Specific behaviors are assessed, not labels

l0. The elapsed time for the process is short

11. Students are treated as human beings and not as irritants or pawns

Summary

The traditional referral and placement process has developed into a bureaucratic process that has proven to be summarily ineffective. Large amounts of time are consumed between the teacher's referral and the initiation of actions placing the child in supplemental programs. Diagnosis, further, has not been educational, rather, it has tended to become a labeling process whereby the children are labeled and whipped off to classrooms of similarly labeled children. The rights of parents and children have often been abused with parents receiving only sketchy knowledge of the referral and placement process.

The traditional format, too, has suffered from ambiguity in behavioral assessment and has tended to be restricted to standardized tests as the major guide in diagnosis. Follow up is vague and evaluation is not a constant process.

The traditional format has suffered from enough problems to ensure that changes were necessary. Given recent court decisions, the process of change in referral and placement has been taken out of the hands of the schools and has been initiated by state government. The new multi-level assessment programs are not abuse proof nor are they infallible. They do offer a viable alternative to the traditional approach and are designed to remove the inequities of the traditional process.

No process can be better than the people that administer and work through the process. The new multi-level approach will either greatly enhance and facilitate the referral and placement process or it will not. As with all programs, it depends on the people conducting the process.

Chapter 5

Placement:
How It Should Work and What Everybody Does

IN THIS chapter we will outline and give specific examples of the placement procedures that we have referred to throughout this text. Separation of the referral process discussed earlier and the placement process to be described here is nearly impossible. Both are complements of each other and are inextricably intertwined in meeting the needs of each child. In this chapter we pick up where the referral process ends, arbitrarily starting with the placement committee.

1. Educational Placement Committee

After the assessment procedure is complete, when all the appropriate data has been gathered and a decision concerning the future of a child's educational program is to be made, a placement committee made up of various people significant in the child's life must be convened in order to determine the educational future of the child. The minimum number of people meeting with the committee should include: (1) The assessment person that has been most closely associated with the evaluation. This, depending on the nature of the problem, may be the school psychologist, the guidance counselor, the social worker, or physician, or any other person most closely involved with the evaluation. (2) The child's current teacher or teachers should under all circumstances be included. If more than one teacher is involved, as in a high school, all should attend at least the initial meeting. (3) The child's potential teacher should also be included. This may be, depending on the assessment process that has previously been in effect, the teacher of the next grade level, or a special education teacher. (4) The child's parent, parents, or legal guardians must be included. (5) The child should be included, if possible.

A description of the responsibilities of each of these individuals follows in short order. Before we examine the group's rights, responsibilities, and functions, however, let us drop back a little bit and summarize the actions that preceed the formation of the placement committee.

A. Referral

Referral, as described in chapter one, was initiated either by the overall screening process or by the child's current teacher based on emotional, intellectual, or physical anomalies. The referral process is initiated by the school system superintendent or the superintendent's designate, generally a principal or another administrative officer. Once the referral process has been put in motion, the consent of the child's parents or legal guardians must be obtained before assessment can begin. It is necessary that all communication with the parents or guardians be written in their native tongue (this, of course, includes ethnic or regional dialect). Once the parents or guardians understand the reasons for the referral and assessment process, their permission must be obtained for the assessment process in writing.

B. The Assessment Process

Once parental consent for the assessment process has been obtained, the superintendent or his designate then has the responsibility of setting in motion the assessment process by contacting the appropriate specialist and directing this person to take the necessary steps.

The six components of assessment as outlined in chapter one must be adhered to. The educational assessment program should also include:

(1) Historical information from the child's cumulative record

(2) Estimate of the child's academic ability and functioning, inferred from both teacher-made tests and standardized test instruments.

(3) Observation of the child in non-academic settings. This includes the general school setting outside the classroom and the environment in and around the child's home.

(4) Estimates of the child's academic and social functioning as determined by the child's parents or other adults that are close to the child.

The assessment process must take into account the child's chronological age, the level of development the child has reached, the cultural background of the child, and the appropriateness of the evaluation instruments or techniques that are used. If a child's home language is any language other than English, the evaluation must be conducted in the child's language or, at least, the English evaluation must be augmented by the native language assessment.

The assessment results must be summarized and reported in writing, containing the signature of all professional personnel involved in the assessment. This report must include:

(1) a description of the assessment procedures

(2) an analysis of the results

(3) specific educational recommendations in detail

(4) specific educational objectives for the child

(5) an estimate of the length of time necessary for the child to meet these objectives.

C. Parental Involvement

Prior to, and during the assessment process, the parents or legal guardians of the child must be informed and included in the operation in several ways. Prior to the initiation of the assessment process, the following steps should be taken and documented by the school systems:

(1) All communication between the school system and the parents must be in the native language of the parents. (This includes regional and ethnic dialects. Written or oral communication in technical jargonese is disallowed. It is expected that technical terms and phrases will not be referred to. Obfuscation, long the hiding place for many of us, is not appropriate in communication with parents.)

(2) The parents will be notified that their child has been referred for assessment and shall be notified as to the source and reasons for the referral. The purpose of the referral must be as clearly stated as possible.

(3) The instruments, devices, or techniques to be used in the assessment process must be fully and clearly described to the parents. Technical jargon should not be used and the emphasis of the description should be on clarity and succinctness, not on flowery technical phraseology.

(4) A realistic timetable delineating the beginning and end of the assessment process and the date at which the educational program shall be chosen for the child must be developed and provided the parents. Adherence to the timetable should be consistent with changes posted to the parents as well as the school personnel.

(5) The right of the parents to accept or reject the assessment and educational program must be clearly and fully related to the parents. Their options must be clearly delineated and the parents must then decide whether or not their child is to be assessed. If they decide in favor of the process, permission by them must be granted in writing.

(6) All records that are kept of the assessment process shall be accessible to the parents. Local school districts should have a person trained in assessment procedures available when parents ask for the data. This person should provide the proper evaluation and interpretation of the data to the parents. In any event no

records such as intelligence test scores, achievement test scores, written teacher reports, and the like can be kept from the parents regardless of the presence or absence of a person to interpret these scores.

(7) The reports of the assessment process, whether interim or final, cannot be distributed for any purpose until the parents are given a copy of the report. The parents have the right to raise questions, clear up points that are fuzzy, and to add whatever material they feel is relevant. If disagreements between the parents and the written report are large, the parents may provide a different report from their point of view, in writing, if they choose. Further, the decision as to who may see the written evaluation is to be made by the parents. The schools may not distribute the reports or any information contained in the reports without the permission of the parents.

(8) If the parents steadfastly refuse assessment or placement when, in the judgement of the school, it is essential to the well-being of the student, the school should collect all information concerning the student currently available, prepare a specific document describing the necessity of placement, record the parental refusal, and forward the material to the superintendent of schools.

D. Responsibilities of the Placement Committee

The committee, after the assessment process, has the general responsibility of working for the maximum benefit of the child. Each member of the committee should prepare not only the data gathered in the assessment process for use in the meeting, but also whatever pertinent comments and suggestions that can be adapted for determining the child's academic future. The major responsibility of the committee is to formulate the best possible educational program available to the child. The committee must, in this process, determine goals and objectives that are to be met by the child within a six-month period academically and socially, if need be. They must also formulate how the goals and objectives for the child agree or disagree with the educational program he or she will be following.

During the initial committee meeting a decision will be made concerning the educational recommendations for the child. During the second meeting the recommendations will be discussed with the parents and a timetable for meeting short-term and long-term objectives in the placement process shall be agreed upon. The written summary of the recommendations and the timetable shall then be an agreement between the parents and the school system. The recommendations are then forwarded to the superintendent or the person designated by the superintendent for implementation. During that and following meetings concerning the child, parents may, if they choose, bring supplementary professional or legal testimony to add to the meeting.

E. The Timetable

A timetable should be developed by the placement committee for each student including the following components:

(1) continuous re-evaluation meetings

(2) short-term educational goals

(3) long-term educational goals

(4) cessation of special education services (where applicable)

(5) renegotiation dates for the educational program

The timetable as set forth in the original meeting shall be somewhat flexible, but agreements should never exceed two years. Keeping individual variations, logistic problems, illness, and other confounding factors in mind, a margin for error should be included in the timetable. Of course, if the student meets the goals much more rapidly than expected, meetings for further educational placement should be adjusted so as to ensure the student's maximum benefit from the program.

F. An Ongoing Evaluation Process

Evaluation of each student must be a continuous and never ending process. People change, conditions change, programs change, and needs, of course, also change. The only way to ensure that each student receives the best possible education is to evaluate the program the student is in compared to the performance of the child. Placement can only be successful as long as the student's goals and objectives are compatible with the aims and goals of his or her educational program. The process must be a sensitive one, adjusting to meet the student's needs. The adjustments can only be carried out via evaluation.

G. Keeping Parents Informed

Parents must be kept informed of the constant evaluation process. Whatever information is gathered by the school must be shared with the parents. Full disclosure of all the child's activities, behaviors, and academic progress must be made to the parents.

2. Standards for Special Education and Supportive Services

In order to insure that placement is reasonably successful, the special education and supportive services must meet certain minimum standards. The needs of the students must be kept at the forefront of any instructional program. To do this the following four factors must be considered:

(A) Students with different kinds of handicaps may need different educational programs. In each instance, the programs must be fitted to the educational needs of the students. It is possible to place children with different forms of handicaps together if their educational needs are similar. In other words, if grouping is necessary to provide an instructional program, it may be carried out through grouping by handicap or by grouping by educational need.

(B) Objectives for each educational program, regardless of its nature, must be student based. This means that the broad goals of the program must be developed from the individual goals that are devised for each of the students in the program. This is not to say that the program is to be fragmented or uncoordinated, either. Students with similar needs should be grouped together to facilitate the preparation and actions necessary for them to meet their individual goals.

(C) The program objectives must coincide with the objectives developed for each individual student.

(D) The curriculum in each program must be individualized to meet the needs of each child. Individualized instruction, evaluation and assessment are all important factors within the broader scope of the instructional program. The program should be developed (a program for a group of children with similar handicaps) to allow maximum flexibility in the individualization of instruction.

In order to meet these four criteria, the program must be sequential, that is, starting where each individual student is at and moving in ordered steps to the educational goal. The program must be developmentally oriented, taking into account the developmental level of the students physically, emotionally, and intellectually. The program must be goal oriented and committed toward working for individual and program goals. The program must be non-ambiguous and open to the public, i.e., the program should not be obsessed with technical jargon and must be made open for public information. Lastly, the program must be under continuous scrutiny allowing for continuous evaluation and changes and revision based on the evaluation of the programs and of the children's progress in the programs.

Generally speaking all programs must consider the chronological and mental ages of the children as well as their physical and emotional development. This seems to be a very simple caution, but it is a very necessary one. Educational programs that include too wide a variety of students with multi-variate problems and developmental levels are doomed to suffer severe problems if not failure. The lack of proper planning to take into account these individual differences will ordinarily result in poor programs that will be of little aid to anyone.

Mandatory Services

Since all school systems will differ in the make-up of their school populations, the special education and supportive services will also have to differ. In large systems the scope of special services may be very broad including many small subgroupings of children via different possible handicaps. Smaller systems, however, cannot possibly afford all of the wide variety of services but must, as is also the case with the larger systems, provide at least the following special services tailored to meet the needs of the following kinds of handicapped children:

(1) Services must be provided for children with auditory and visual problems as well as those children with physical disabilities or health problems. This, of course, includes "home-bound" or hospital visitation services as well as providing special facilities, equipment and personnel for working with the visually, auditorially, or physically disabled.

(2) Services must be provided for students with speech or language impairments. This, too, includes the necessary specialists, equipment and facilities for a thorough program.

(3) Services must be provided for those students with perceptual, conceptual, sensory, memory, attention, or motor control problems. If the number of students with these various problems is large, then these may be further subdivided according to the students' needs. Again, specialists in these areas must be available as must be the proper equipment, material and facilities to support such a program.

(4) Services must be provided for students with handicaps in intellectual development or mental capacity. Again, if the population of students with such problems is large, the program may be

subdivided by students' needs. Typically, this subdivision should be done according to the individual objectives and goals of groups of students. Facilities, equipment, and specialized personnel must be available to implement the program services.

(5) Where there are students (even if only 1) with educational deficiencies attributable to social or cultural conditions, special services must be provided to rectify these problems. While specialized personnel in this area may be hard to find in large numbers, a staff member with a background in such areas should be assigned to the program and the necessary equipment and facilities provided.

(6) Provision of services for emotionally disturbed children must be included in any school program. This will have to vary from self-contained classes with appropriate personnel and facilities to provisions for counseling and therapy. In cases where therapy is necessary, consultative services of psychologists or psychiatrists should be provided if such a person is not available on a full-time basis. These psychiatric or psychological services should include therapy with the child, parental involvement, family counseling, psychometric assessment, and medical care.

(7) Lastly, and more optimistically, special services should be provided for those students with outstanding academic, creative, or talent abilities. Such programs should be designed to enrich and maximize the chances of these students reaching their optimal potential. Just as special personnel and facilities are necessary for the handicapped students, equally qualified personnel and appropriate materials and facilities must be provided the gifted student.

Although the emphasis of the program as outlined above seems to be providing services for the handicapped, equally good services must be provided for the average or gifted student. Too long in American education, the students that fell outside of the "normative" range have not received the necessary educational services to insure the maximization of their potential. We hope that the specificity of our comments concerning the exceptional child will not attenuate those services provided the average child. Upgrading programs must also include the major portion of our responsibilities: the average student.

H. *Mainstreaming*

The term mainstreaming has recently come to mean the process of keeping children in the normal classroom wherever possible. Indeed, each child should receive his or her education in the normal classroom unless the assessment process has indicated that special classes would be more valuable for the child's educational future and this is agreed to jointly by the school system and the parents.

The burden of proof that a child needs to be placed in special educational classes falls on the school system. The need must be documented and exhaustively investigated by the school system. The school personnel originally involved in the placement process should be available to help initiate the placement procedure.

The special programs that are to be available for children that cannot have their needs met in the normal school must be as similar as is possible to the normal classroom, depending, of course, on the level of severity and the kinds of handicaps. The number of children in such programs should be determined by the age group involved, the level of physical, emotional, and intellectual development, the kind of disability, the severity of the disability, and the amount of special intervention and support necessary to meet the needs of each individual student. Of course, no steadfast rules can be laid down in advance to follow insofar as size of special classes is concerned. Teacher and specialist variables, economic factors, logistics, and the school population all enter into this decision that should be made locally. It is important to point out, however, that these special services should be carried out in the least restrictive possible environment and should be restricted to the shortest length of stay by the child possible in order to meet his or her needs.

3. Options Available to the School System

No one method of providing special educational or supportive services can possibly be considered to be enough to meet the needs of all students that have been identified as needing special services. Several different kinds of options appear to be open to local school systems and we will attempt to identify some of these and describe how they are used. Which programs are essentially chosen, of course, will depend on the needs of the school system in question and the logistics and economics of the specific situation.

(1) The first and, perhaps, most readily available option is that of the normal or regular educational program enhancement with special educational material for students in need of such help. In such a format, the student remains in the normal classroom with his peers and the teacher or the child is given the materials and/or equipment developed to meet his needs. The program is conducted by the regular classroom teacher with guidance from the specialist in that area.

(2) The second option available to the local school system is the regular classroom program augmented with consultative services provided by a special education person. In this program the child again remains in the normal classroom and is provided with special help by the consultant who, along with the regular classroom teacher, implements the program. A consulting teacher should be available in every school. This person should be available to write individualized programs and analyze the data generated thereby. Such a person should serve from between ten and twenty classrooms depending on the number of children involved.

This option, as can easily be inferred, necessitates the presence of a specially trained person as the consulting teacher. The consulting teacher must be an ombudsman capable of many of the tasks normally performed by the special education teacher, the guidance counselor, and the school psychologist. Currently, such a training program as "consulting teacher" does not exist, but as we will relate in chapter seven, the necessity for such a multi-disciplinary program certainly exists and can be easily provided within current practices and curriculum.

(3) The third option is that of providing itinerant special education personnel for special supportive services in the classroom. In this format the special education person visits the classroom and provides direct instruction to those children whose needs can be met with such part-time support.

The itinerant personnel should, of course, meet the training and degree requirements of other certified special education personnel in similar areas of instruction, e.g., those personnel providing itinerant services for the perceptually handicapped should hold the same qualifications as those personnel in self-contained programs for the perceptually handicapped. The ratio of children to itinerant personnel should be ten to one. The effectiveness of itinerant personnel would be greatly diminished if the ratio exceeded ten or twelve to one.

These special itinerant programs should be designed and implemented so as to minimize disruption of the normal classroom. The itinerant personnel and the classroom teacher should work closely together in planning and developing educational goals for the children involved in the itinerant program.

(4) The fourth option consists of augmenting the regular classroom with special instruction outside the regular classroom for less than one-half of the day. In such a program the child attends the regular program for more than half the schoolday and spends the remainder of the day with a special resource or special education teacher. The special program must be designed to meet the needs of the students as determined by the kind of handicap or problem they have and the amount of intervention necessary for the children.

Such instruction may be provided individually or in small groups, depending on the nature of the school's population. However the education is provided, it must be carefully integrated with the regular classroom program. Communication between the special teacher and the regular classroom teacher should be frequent and consistent allowing for the maximization of efforts.

The teacher-child ratio for such a program should be close to 10 to 20 children per teacher, depending on the handicap and the levels of severity of the handicaps. Such a program, naturally, could be a dual purpose program servicing one group of children in the first part of the day and a second group in the latter half of the day. If the program is implemented on this group basis, of course, a self-contained classroom unit should be provided as well as all the necessary materials and equipment.

(5) The fifth option available to the local school system is the use of the regular classroom to augment the special educational program. This is the first of the programs, so far, that emphasizes the normal classroom as a support to the special educational program. In this program the child remains in the normal classroom less than half a day. The rest of the day is spent with the resource teacher either individually or in a small group situation.

The length of stay in the special program should be determined by the nature and scope of the handicap. Care must be taken so that the child's experiences in the normal and special classes are congruent and complement each other. Communication, of course, is still a necessary part of the program in order to allow both the normal and special classes to maximize their level of service.

A self-contained classroom is necessary for such a program along with whatever materials and equipment are needed. The children should be grouped according to their special needs and educational objectives. The teacher-student ratio should run closely to one to twelve for each such educational center in the school, e.g., one special resource or education teacher for every twelve visually handicapped children and one special teacher for every twelve emotionally handicapped children. In large schools, where the need is determined, this may mean several such self-contained units and resource teachers.

(6) The sixth option to be described is an unusual one and generally will not effect a large number of children. The option, regular or special school services combined with supplemental services furnished by public or private outside agencies, provides that the majority of the child's educational experience be provided by the normal classroom or the special educational services, and that the child receive whatever special help that he or she needs from outside agencies.

Such programs can be psychiatric, e.g., private psychiatrists, regional mental health centers and community agencies; physically therapeutic, e.g., local clinics or special organizations; or any other service wherein the student's needs are best met by outside agencies.

(7) Option number seven, a full-time special educational program, is the option wherein a child receives the bulk of his educational experiences via individualized instruction in special classes. These experiences should be complemented where possible by experiences in the regular classroom or appropriate supportive services in and out of the school.

Complete facilities must be provided for such programs and the teacher to pupil ratio should be near one teacher to ten students. The students, of course, should be grouped according to their ages, developmental levels and handicaps.

(8) The eighth option, special day schools, is that option designed to serve students that are so severely handicapped that services within the schools cannot meet their needs. These special day schools may be public or private.

(9) Option nine is the special residential school, a school for children so severely handicapped that public schools and special day schools cannot accommodate the needs of these children.

(10) The tenth option is that of the visiting teacher. This option denotes that on occasion children may need instruction either in a hospital or at home during illnesses. The visiting teacher must be

academically and professionally certified to teach at the same level as the normal classroom teacher.

These options, of course, do not exhaust the possible forms of educational services for children in need of special help. They are offered only as examples of possible programs. Each state will naturally have guidelines somewhat different from other states and from the general guidelines that we have provided. The point of the matter, however, is to demonstrate possibilities, not final answers.

Support Services

Support services include a broad spectrum of services not generally considered academic in nature. The support services that should be provided in any school include school psychological services, guidance and counseling services, social work services, health services, and attendance services. In this section we will delineate the responsibilities of people in each of these areas. The emphasis, naturally, should be on prevention, but large portions of the programs should also center on rehabilitation and direct services.

(1) School Psychological Services

School psychological services should be provided all children in the school system. The school psychologist should help facilitate a climate within the school so as to optimize the development of all the children. The prime function of the school psychological service is psychological evaluation and assistance in education, emotional or behavioral adjustment.

In general, the school psychological services should include screening of school populations in order to identify those children who should be referred for individual study; interpretations of psychological evaluations of individual children and recommendations that lead to appropriate and relevant educational experiences for the child; counseling, therapy, or other remedial psychological actions in order to meet the needs of the students either individually or in groups; meeting with parents and engaging in public relations; parental counseling and parental education; functioning as teacher consultants for behavior management and learning problems; and engaging in program development with other school personnel.

(2) Guidance and Counseling Services

Counseling services should be designed to deal with the counseling and guidance needs of all children in a school. It should be a service that helps and supports the general educational program. The responsibilities of the counselor include assisting in identifying those children in need of special help; evaluating children in need of special help and identifying whatever sources are available to help meet these children's needs; orienting children and parents to the school and the services and programs available at the school; counseling children, parents, and other concerned adults either individually or in groups; collecting, colating, and maintaining data gathered from students to be used in evaluating and planning educational programs for the children; helping in the placement process of children; and providing counseling services to assist children in developing accurate self-concepts, making personnel adjustments, making vocational and career choices and evaluating personal abilities while enhancing the maximization of their use and growth.

(3) School Social Services

School social services, the province of the school social worker, is that facet of the support services designed to aid children with problems in the home or neighborhood environment. School social services should include consultative and in-service training with other school personnel; identifying those children in need of special services; serving children and/or their homes directly; serving parents and in this manner serving the children by providing parental counseling and education; and developing community relations and using the resources of the community to meet the needs of children or helping develop new community service programs.

(4) School Health Services

Health services basically provide the school population with health care needed to maximize the well-being of students. The responsibilities of the health services include recognizing health problems that may harm a child's educational or developmental growth via screening; interpreting health needs and following them up; accurately maintaining and evaluating health records; providing for accident prevention and disease control; keeping tabs on children in school that must use medication; and providing background information and the appropriate consultations for members of the school staff working with children that have health problems.

(5) Attendance Services

Attendance services generally deal only with the narrow scope of school attendance by children. The responsibilities of the attendance personnel include identifying problems or factors that impede a child's school attendance; finding solutions for attendance problems or helping meet children's needs that are related to attendance problems; and developing a good working relationship between the home and the school.

(6) Other Support Services

There are four other supportive services that should be offered through the school. Special reading services should be provided for those children that are having difficulties in the area of reading. The reading personnel, certainly, must be certified in reading. Services for those children with visual or hearing problems must be provided. This supportive service should include personnel trained in braille, typing instructors, and interpreters for deaf or auditorally impaired children. Physical therapy support services must be provided for those children in need of the services. Lastly, special consultative services must be provided for those children whose needs fall outside the scope of the school's abilities to meet them.

The nine support services we have described do not meet all students' needs, nor are they in any way a final answer as to what each individual school must be restricted to. Each school will have rather special populations with special needs. Supportive services must be geared to meet the needs of the students and in so doing must, of necessity, vary from the examples that we provided.

Standards of Eligibility

Each child's eligibility for special education services and programs should be determined in a staff meeting with all concerned members of the staff from multiple disciplines present. The decision should be based on a thorough evaluative assessment process that has generated the necessary amount of appropriate data for this kind of decision.

There are four basic categories of children that should be eligible. These are described below:

(1) All children whose educational needs cannot be met in regular programs without augmentation by enrichment or special materials, equipment, or supportive personnel are eligible.

(2) All children whose educational needs cannot be met without supportive teachers, either special educators, resource teachers, or itinerant teachers, are eligible for these services.

(3) Any children with handicaps, from one to several, that are severe enough to justify a continuous process of intensive, specialized intervention are eligible for these services.

(4) Any child with a handicap that will cause absence from school for two weeks or more is eligible for the visiting teacher program.

Summary

In this chapter we have attempted to outline the necessary services a school should provide for any children in need of special services. We have discussed the educational placement committee and outlined the role of this committee with respect to referral, assessment, parental involvement, timetable development, and the continuing evaluation process.

The standards for special educational and support services were outlined with reference to instructional programs, student objectives, program objectives, individualization of experience, necessary components of the curriculum, accountable instruction factors, services that must be provided by the school system, and mainstreaming.

Each of the options that are representations of special and supportive services were discussed, listing the necessary components of each.

Supportive services were examined and some guidelines governing the various services were outlined. Finally, standards of eligibility for students were discussed.

In this chapter we could only roughly approximate the kinds of programs that each individual school may need. Regardless of the variations that exist from system to system, the major point we want to make is that the rights and needs of students must be met and that it is the responsibility of the school system to do so.

CASE HISTORY INFORMATION
(Classroom Teacher)

Date: _____

Student's Name: _____

Consultant's Name: _____

Reading:

Math:

Spelling:

Writing:

Behavior:

Subject Matter Area	Personal & Social Development
Arithmetic	Conduct ....
Art.............................	Accepts & completes responsibility
Bible	Considerate of others...........
Health & Safety	Cooperates in Group Work.......
Language	Follows Directions ....
Music	Neatness ....
Penmanship	Completes Assignments ....
Reading	
Social Studies	
Science.........................	
Spelling.........................	_____
	Teacher's Name

Final Follow-up Form—Resource Consultant
(To be completed by classroom teacher)

Student's Name: .... Date: ....

Has this child shown improvement in his rate of progress in your class since your initial contact with the Resource Consultant?

Marked Improvement ☐   Some Improvement ☐   No Improvement ☐

Areas	Comments
Reading	....
Spelling........................	....
Penmanship	....
Arithmetic	....
Arithmetic	....
Classroom Conduct	....
Self-Concept	....
Most recent or predicted grade reports:	Approx. date of report ....

Subject Matter Area	Personal & Social Development
Arithmetic	Conduct ....
Art.............................	Accepts responsibility ....
Health & Safety	Considerate of others ....
Language	Cooperates in Group Work ......
Music	Follows Directions ....
Penmanship	Neatness ....
Reading	Completes Assignments ....
Social Studies	
Science........................	
Spelling........................	....
	Teacher's Name

(To be completed by Resource Consultant after conference with Classroom Teacher)

Comments and Recommendations: ....
....

....
        Date   Resource Consultant's Name

INDIVIDUAL PROGRAMMING

Date: _____

Student's Name: _____

Consultant's Name: _____

Resource Program	Teacher Program	Parent Program
. . . .	. . . .	. . . .
. . . .	. . . .	. . . .
. . . .	. . . .	. . . .
. . . .	. . . .	. . . .

INDIVIDUAL PROGRAMMING

Date _____

Student's Name: _____

Consultant's Name: _____

Weaknesses	Strengths	Date	Obj. Eval.	Objectives
. . . .	. . . .	. . . . . .	. . . .	. . . .
. . . .	. . . .	. . . . . .	. . . .	. . . .
. . . .	. . . .	. . . . . .	. . . .	. . . .
. . . .	. . . .	. . . . . .	. . . .	. . . .

CONTACT SHEETS

Student's Name_____ School_____

Consultant's Name_____ Contact Nos._____

Contact #___	Conference			Diag.			Diag.	Follow-	
	Par	Tchr	Other	Obs.	Testing	Teaching	Prog.	up	Other
Date___									
		Comment:							

Contact #___	Conference			Diag.			Diag.	Follow-	
	Par	Tchr	Other	Obs.	Testing	Teaching	Prog.	up	Other
Date___									
		Comment:							

Contact #___	Conference			Diag.			Diag.	Follow-	
	Par	Tchr	Other	Obs.	Testing	Teaching	Prog.	up	Other
Date___									
		Comment:							

FOLLOW-UP REPORT
Consulting Teacher

Child's Name _____

Date _____   No. of Contacts _____

Additional Materials: ....
....
....
Results: ....
....
....
Recommendations: ....
....
....
Notes: ....
....
....
....

_____
Consulting Teacher

CASE HISTORY INFORMATION

Student's Name_____ **B/D**_____

Consultant's Name_____ **Date**_____

Psychological and/or referral summary: ....
....
....

Hearing Screening .... Recommendations ....
....
Follow-up: ....
....
Vision Screening.......... Recommendations ....
....
Follow-up: ....
....

Data from Cumulative Record: ....
....
....

_____
Teacher

Chapter **6**

After Placement: Individualized Instruction

THIS CHAPTER deals with one of the most complex areas of education: individualized instruction. During this chapter we will discuss the following:

1. The behavioral objective

2. Evaluation, norm-referenced vs. criterion referenced

3. Kinds of instructional programs

4. Developing individualized instruction

    a. statements of what is to be learned

    b. behavioral objectives

    c. learning activities and materials

    d. evaluation

We cannot offer a complete description of all the possible areas of interest to the reader as this area is one that has experienced an explosion of knowledge in recent years. We will attempt to develop a general discussion of all these areas and provide realistic examples throughout the chapter.

1. The Behavioral Objective

In any program of individualized instruction, the key to success will be the proper use of behavioral objectives (Mager, 1962). We have all heard a considerable amount of talk concerning the use of behavioral objectives but many of us either do not use them, or if we do, we use them improperly. Let us investigate the necessary components of a behavioral objective, carry one example through the process of developing the behavioral objective, and discuss the reasons why behavioral objectives are valuable and why they are superior to non-behaviorally stated objectives.

Mager (1962) describes the process of formulating objectives as a process that defines the change in behavior of a student in an absolutely unequivocal manner, i.e., a manner that cannot be misconstrued, misunderstood, or misrepresented by the instructor, the student, or anyone else presented with the objective. From Mager's description, we see an objective as a statement describing the change in behavior of a student. (Incidentally, it might interest the reader to know that the most generally acceptable definition of learning is a semi-permanent change in behavior. Hence, objectives are designed to describe the outcome of learning in terms of the change in behavior of the learner). This objective, the description of change in a student's behavior, must have three necessary components (Mager, 1962).

A. The change in behavior must be behaviorally specified in unambiguous terms, i.e., the behavior must be specified in observable, measurable and replicable terms. This means that terms such as "appreciate," "understand," "grasp the significance of" and other professorial favorites will have to be discarded. After all, how can we measure such a thing as "appreciate"?

We have experienced certain collegiate professors who administered tests that were supposed to measure our "appreciation" of English literature with 70 item multiple choice exams. (This might not have been so bad in itself, but the questions all seemed to be written in Sanskrit. Naturally, all areas, not just English literature, produce such wonderful exams.) In other words, terms such as "appreciate" or "understand" cannot be measured. "Appreciate" to some students means to memorize, to others it may mean to recognize, and to still others, "appreciate" may mean no more than to be aware of the existence of the appreciable material in question. As an example, if we ask if the reader understands what has just been written, no doubt the answer would be yes. But what if we measure this understanding with a test that forces total recall? You see, any verb form that is not an action verb that can be "seen in action," so to speak, is almost useless.

The action verbs that can be observed, measured, and replicated include verbs such as list, write, identify, construct, and so on. Each of these verbs is relatively unambiguous. If our objective over the material in this chapter were for the reader to list the three components of a behavior objective, there could be no ambiguity in the objective. We can easily (if we were physically present) observe the listing behavior (that is, either the listing occurs or it does not) and identify to what extent it occurs, i.e., one component, two components, or three components. Further, we can measure the listing behavior in terms of speed, accuracy and completeness. We can also easily replicate the behavior. The inclusion of a verb form that can be observed, measured, and replicated is the most important aspect of the behavioral objective.

B. The conditions under which the new behavior is to be measured must be included in the formally stated behavioral objective. In other words, is the objective to be met on a teacher made test, as part of a larger behavioral pattern, on standardized instruments, or in actual practice? A student should prepare rather differently for demonstrating mastery of an objective on a teacher made test than, for instance, demonstrating mastery in an oral recitation in front of 100 people in an auditorium.

A further reason for specifying conditions under which mastery of an objective is to be measured is to guide the instructor in devising teaching techniques designed to help the student meet the objective in the situation in which the objective will be measured. Certainly we might alter our teaching techniques (at least we should) if we are going to use a discussion exam to measure our students' mastery of objectives as opposed to the use of multiple choice or true and false examinations. So, the second component of our behavioral objective becomes the conditions under which the behavior we have specified will be measured.

C. The third component of the behavioral objective must be the criteria for acceptance of objective mastery. In other words, must all three components be listed for us to accept the objective as having been met, or will we accept two out of the three for an acceptable level of the behavior? If we are measuring identification with a multiple choice test, must the student identify 70, 80, or 90 percent of the items? The criteria for behaviors that meet objectives will differ from behavior to behavior. Obviously if we want a child to verbalize the sound of the letter M every time we show the letter, the criteria have little flexibility. The person on the spot, however, may determine that a 90-percent accuracy level is acceptable and go on to the next objective.

The example: Let us hypothetically develop one behavioral objective for a child that is learning disabled. Obviously, before we can decide upon the appropriateness or inappropriateness of any objective, we must determine the current levels of behavior from the child we are working with (a further discussion of this immediately follows this section). After a determination of what behaviors are present and what new behaviors the child should master has been made, we may then move to the process of developing concrete behavioral objectives.

The art of writing behavioral objectives is a never ending process. Working with any individual child, we may postulate what we feel are objectives that logically follow the assessment of current behaviors. Individual differences, however, will ensure that some students will meet our objectives very rapidly while others may never reach them. Hence, the first aspect of objective development is the individuality of the process of developing objectives. This may mean a process of readjusting objectives that are out of the reach of students to some level within their reach. Further, it denotes that some objectives can never be met by some people. For instance, few of us could ever replicate the mathematical proofs behind Einstein's theory of relativity, regardless of how much instruction or training we were to receive. Objectives must be developed, as Drumheller (1971) points out, within the ability level of the student. The process of adequately preparing an objective within the ability level of a student is difficult. It is a process that often becomes trial and error until the instructor becomes familiar enough with the student so that he or she can use a systematic process developed from the earlier trial and error experience.

We are assuming now that we have adequately gauged the ability level of the student and that our objective will be within the ability level of the student. Joe, our hypothetical student, cannot discriminate between the letters b and d. We feel, however, that this is within his ability level as he adequately discriminates between n and m, p and q, and s and z. Our objective, then, becomes a matter of having Joe discriminate between b and d at some acceptable level. Let us state this in a behavioral fashion.

Joe will say the name for the letter b when it is pointed to by the teacher. Since we have a dichotomous sort of objective, it is necessary to provide the complement of the previous objective.

Joe will say the name for the letter d when it is pointed to by the teacher. Notice that there is no ambiguity in the verb form chosen for these two objectives. That is, it can certainly be observed (we listen), measured (either it happens or it does not, and it happens at some frequency level) and it is easily replicable (we can ask for a repeat performance).

We must further refine our objective, however, to meet the necessary criteria for a complete objective. We must set forth the conditions under which the behavior is to occur. When this is taken into account, our objective becomes:

> Joe will say the name for the letter b when it is pointed to by the teacher on a large sheet containing many letters. This will be done in the classroom during the reading period.

Our objective now gives Joe and the teacher the parameters within which the behavior must occur. (There are, of course, many other possibilities for this, but we use this only as an example.) This gives all those involved in the teaching/learning process an unambiguous set of conditions under which the behavior must occur.

Well, at what level of performance will Joe's behavior be seen as acceptable? Must Joe correctly identify b's and d's 50 percent of the time, 90 percent of the time, 100 percent of the time? This is a decision that must be based on the individual student's abilities and needs, the form of objective that we are working with, the part the objective plays in the overall educational objective, and the final educational objective itself. Based on such considerations, we might believe that a 95-percent accuracy performance level would meet the objective in terms of Joe's performance. This gives us our objective (really a pair of dichotomous objectives) in its final form:

> Joe will say the name for the letter b when it is pointed to by the teacher on a large sheet containing many letters at a 95-percent level of accuracy. This will be done in the classroom during the reading period.

As can be seen, it isn't strictly necessary to refine the objective to the point of over-kill. Once conditions are decided upon, likely as not, the need for continuing to state them will become redundant. There is no substitute, however, for the action verb and the criteria. They must, in each instance, be stated.

Assessment. The assessment process in individualized instruction programs is a constant process that begins when the child is assessed at the onset of entering school and does not end until the child leaves school. After objectives have been defined, the process, as we have noted, is a rather smooth one with the evaluation built directly into the process of defining objectives. The initial assessment process, of course, is the one we defined in an earlier chapter.

2. Norm Referenced vs. Criterion Referenced Evaluation

Norm referenced evaluation, as the term implies, is evaluation that is referenced by a norm group. At this point it is probably necessary that we describe the process of norm referencing more fully so as to clarify the terms we will be using. Norm referenced evaluation can be based upon the functioning of a normative group (Perkins, 1972). A normative group is a group that is a sample of some population that reflects to a high degree of accuracy the qualities of the total population. For example, if our population is all the third graders in the United States, the reference group would be a sample chosen (chosen either randomly or with certain kinds of techniques so as to guarantee that the qualities of the sample group are similar to the population) to represent the entire population of third graders. Hence, if there were one million third graders we might choose three or four thousand of these children to represent the whole group. The reference group would then be assessed over whatever variables the investigator was interested in and a series of performance scores and percentiles would be computed to allow us to examine any one child or any group of children and compare them to the reference group.

This whole process is built around the idea of "normal" or "norm" performance. The figure on page 113 represents a typical normal probability curve. As can be seen from this figure, the majority of students obtained scores between 85 and 115 (68%). Very few students fall above or below this range of scores. A quick inspection of the figure, however, tells us that exactly half of the students fall above the mean and the other half fall below it.

In examining this table we would compare our student's score with the scores in the table. The percentages alongside each score represent the percentage of the sample that scored at or below the student's score, providing some idea of where our student falls compared to the norm group. For example, a score of about 80 would mean that our hypothetical student would have scored at a level at or above 20% of the normal population.

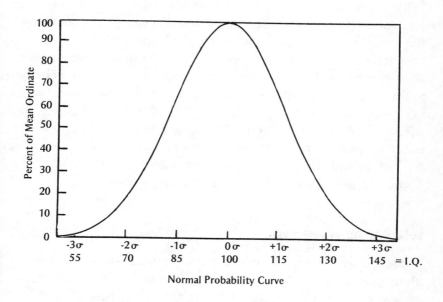

Normal Probability Curve

Regardless of the population we examine or the variable we choose to examine, the parameters will be the same. Our norm referenced evaluation will compare our child or group of children to national norms on some measures. Unfortunately, however, there are many more times when norm referenced evaluation is inappropriate. For example, if a child scores in the fifth percentile at the beginning of the school year and again at the end of the year, it appears as though there has been no improvement, when in fact, remaining at the fifth percentile indicates that the student had to at least stay abreast with the level of improvement of the entire group.

Another problem with norm referenced tests is the fact that students in disadvantaged areas, although scoring very well in comparison to other students in their area, score poorly when compared to the national norms.

Perhaps the largest failing of the norm referenced system is the emphasis on what the majority of the group is doing or can do.

What sense does it make to evaluate a child in terms of a normal population if the child is learning disabled? Perhaps the solution to the problem lies in criterion referenced evaluation. In criterion referenced evaluation there is no normative group and no reference is made to a normal group. All references are to the change in the student's behavior measured prior to and after some teaching or training techniques. This implies, of course, that the student's capabilities are taken into account and that the criteria for success amount to the student meeting those goals set for him. As McClelland (1973) points out, there must be alternatives to the norm referenced kinds of evaluations that we seem to be bogged down in.

What is Normal?

Basic to the norm referenced form of evaluation is the concept of normality. We all know what's "normal." What's normal is what's good for you, it's the way to act or the best kind of performance. Is normality really this? Some men are six feet tall. This is an inoccuous statement, one that seems rather silly and superficial. Yet, any American male six feet tall or taller is abnormal. How can this be? We would all like to think of our sons growing to be six feet tall or taller. Isn't it good to be six feet tall? Well, maybe it is and maybe it isn't, but the idea of good and bad has absolutely nothing to do with the concept of normality. The obvious thing to be gleaned from this is that what is abnormal or not normal is not necessarily bad. Remember when we pointed out above that exactly half of the students fall above the norm? That wasn't just an idle statement. If we interpret normality in the strictest sense, almost the entire population would be abnormal. Normality is a statistical concept that, in common parlance, has gained the meaning of something good or worthwhile. In fact, what is good or worthwhile is not often what is normal. We would all like our children to be more intelligent than normal, our incomes to be higher than normal, and our cigarette intake to be less than normal. Normality is merely a concept designed to describe a population of individuals in statistical fashion concerning whatever is being measured. Being abnormal, not normal, is not the same as being bad. The connotations that the term normality has gained from association with mental health or with physical health are not appropriate to the purpose of evaluating a child's progress.

The key word above was progress. We cannot compare the ability levels of retarded and "normal" children for obvious reasons. Just as obviously, we cannot compare progress between two such individuals. For the retarded child, the identification of the letter L may be a very exciting attainment whereas our "normal" child may really not be striving much to read ten novels in the same period of time.

Criterion Referenced Evaluation

Criterion referenced evaluation, as we pointed out earlier, measures a student's progress as compared to his abilities and the amount of effort the student expends in attaining his goal. All references to change in the student's behavior deal with the change measured after some learning activity. The goals must be realistic and reflect whatever capabilities the student has. It is, indeed, necessary for us to recognize that for some students the attainment of self-toileting behavior will be a very great accomplishment while others may really not be taxed by developing the proofs behind Einstein's theory of relativity. In summary, criterion referenced evaluation stresses the individual's abilities, his abilities to change and the amount of change he has achieved with respect to his personal background. Success in criterion referenced evaluation is attainment of reasonable, personal goals. It is truly an individualized form of evaluation.

When Norm Referenced Evaluation is Used.

When norm referenced evaluation is deemed desirable by the school personnel, five basic guidelines should be followed to insure that normative evaluation becomes a worthwhile evaluation. First, the population to be evaluated should be succinctly and completely specified while at the same time the norm group should also be fully described. Secondly, only fully qualified personnel should be involved in administering and evaluating the test. Third, the tests or specific tasks and items from the tests should be very carefully selected to guarantee their appropriateness for the group to be evaluated. Accordingly, such factors as age, sex, socioeconomic status, and cultural backgrounds of the pupils should guide this process. Fourth, administration should be uniform and proper measures should be taken to insure the validity of the procedures. Fifth, evaluation should never be based solely on results from standardized instruments.

A final comment concerning norm referenced and criterion referenced evaluation seems necessary. Either of the two forms, or the two forms in combination may be used. The purpose, of course, is to provide the best possible evaluation of each student in order to maximize the learning process. Norm referenced evaluation may be used to locate the level at which instructional objectives and strategies should start, or, if commercially produced materials are used, to delineate the level and kinds of materials to be purchased. In other words, norm referenced evaluations may provide the school personnel with the "starting place" at which to further evaluate the students. Criterion referenced evaluation, of course, must be used to determine the level to which objectives are attained and the progress of individual students.

3. Kinds of Instructional Programs

Gibbons (1971) classifies several different forms of individualized instruction programs according to the manner in which the systems are organized. His basic forms of instructional programs are active, responsive, and permissive. In this section we will briefly describe each of these forms and then further subdivide individualized instruction programs.

Active programs and permissive programs are at the extremes. In active programs the assumption is made that there is a specifiable body of knowledge to be learned and that the major decisions are to be made by the instructor with only the rate of learning prescribed by the students' needs (Jordan, 1967). Permissive programs, on the other hand, assume that all relevant decisions concerning content, pacing, method of evaluation, structure of knowledge, and teaching/learning style can be and should be made by the student (Gleason, 1967).

These two forms of individualized instruction differ rather dramatically in philosophical as well as practical terms. Though we could engage in a long discourse contrasting the two forms, we will only state that either can be very efficient given the proper personnel and materials, and in the case of the permissive format, capable enough students to choose appropriate learning experiences. For the purposes of our discussion, however, we are most interested in those students that do not easily meet the requirements of either permissive or active programs. We generally are advocates of individualized instruction for any student or group of students for whom both the content and the specificity of the content must be determined.

To fill the needs of the special students we have been dealing with, it is necessary to compromise between the active and permissive modes of individualized instruction. The combination of these two modes is generally referred to as the responsive mode of individualized instruction (Gibbons, 1971). The responsive mode allows the teacher to choose the appropriate content, environment, and teaching techniques. The student may choose (or have chosen for him, depending on the severity of the learning problem) the kinds of materials he works with best and the rate at which he will progress. Responsive individualized programs allow a constant feedback loop to exist between the teacher and the student, providing for constant evaluation and re-evaluation not only of the mastery of the material but also the preferences of materials and the appropriateness of the techniques in use. The responsive mode is best characterized by the cooperative nature of the decision-making process for the learning situation.

The three kinds of instruction we have just mentioned can further be subdivided into individual or group administration techniques. Group approaches to individualized instruction amount to providing some group, selected either from common needs, problems, or goals, with the same "individualized" program for each member of the group. Time of mastery is usually the only factor that separates the students, the only individualization factor. The group administration technique is not well suited to the wide range of student needs likely to appear in our special programs. Gibbons (1971) goes so far as to say that group approaches may involve such small changes from traditional approaches that they may become excuses for the problems they pretend to solve. In light of this and other, similar comments concerning group approaches (Cremin, 1961; Gleason, 1967; Kapfer and Ovard, 1972) we will not long dwell on what has been regarded as a poor approach to individualized instruction. Our only comment, then, is that if nothing else save the traditional format is available, grouping for individualized instruction may be attempted but the philosophical and practical compromises promise a rather dubious outcome at best.

Individualized individual instruction is probably what the reader has in mind when he or she thinks of individualized instruction. In practical terms it means that the teacher deals with each individual separately from every other individual. Co-operative decisions are made concerning each student's needs and the teacher is literally administering eight or ten dissimilar educational programs based on the needs of each student.

The last form of categorization that we will mention (although subdivisions are possible to a much greater degree even though the divisions mean less and less each time) is the distinction between direct and indirect programs. Direct instruction programs are those that involve the teacher directly with each student at the request of either the student or the teacher. The indirect form of program is one in which the teacher is only indirectly involved and in which the majority of decisions are made by the student. From these various forms of individualized instruction programs, we will describe the development of a responsive, individual, and direct form of individualized instruction program.

Commercial Programs

The market in educational materials has recently been swamped with a virtual avalanche of "individualized instructional materials." The materials are called by many different names and have different kinds of configurations. Some are better than others. Some are cheaper than others. Some are for college level students and some are for the elementary students. Regardless of all the possible variations among the commercial learning packages, they all share a common fault. The common fault is that they cannot possibly be tailored for the needs of each individual student, even though some are designed for changes. Relative to a school's resources, commercial programs are expensive and wasteful. Total individualized instruction demands just exactly what its name implies: total individualized instruction. This is just not possible with commercial materials for special children no matter how good the materials are. Until such a time as we are convinced that commercial programs have developed to the point that the needs of all possible children can be filled by a commercial program, we will counsel against the use of commercial programs for the developmentally, emotionally, or mentally retarded child. (Incidentally, many of the commercial materials available are excellent when used appropriately with "normal" school children from kindergarten through the graduate level. We are not attempting to alienate the writers and publishers of the commercial materials, but we feel rather strongly about meeting the needs of the children that are in our special education classes and programs.)

4. Developing Individualized Instruction

What are the components of individualized instruction? Very basically, there are four components of any individualized learning program. These components are (A) the concept, skill, or value to be learned, (B) specified behavior objectives, (C) learning activities and materials designed to meet the objectives and (D) evaluation (Drumheller, 1971). In this section we will examine each of these components in detail and develop an example of a very simple learning package.

A. What Is To Be Learned/Taught?

As Kapfer and Ovard (1972) point out, any judgement as to what the student is to learn will be a value judgement. It becomes the job of the writer of individualized instruction programs to sort, re-sort, throw away, replace, and find the most relevant things to be taught to each individual child. To further complicate matters, things to be learned can be classed into concepts, conceptual abstractions that are learned through cognitive processes; skills, psychomotor activities learned through physical practice and cognitive processes; and values, abstract ideas or concepts that denote affective behaviors and changes in affective behaviors. As the reader can see, these three categories of things to be learned are very oversimplified with a considerable amount of overlap on any given thing to learn. There is also the problem of specifying any of these three categories to anyone's satisfaction. However, any new bit of knowledge to be acquired really contains parts of all three of the categories we mentioned (Kapfer and Ovard, 1972). Whatever concept, skill, or value is to be learned, the teacher in the special class has the choice of deciding what areas to teach and how to go about teaching this knowledge.

What is important? This is the single question that should guide the teacher in determining what to cover. No two teachers will make the same decisions in exactly the same way, but referral to developmental skills and knowledge describing normative groups should ease some of these problems.

Why bother to write out the concepts that we wish to teach if all these problems are involved? Why not just decide what is to be taught and go on about our business? The reason we include the written concepts in the individualized program is very simple: The same word used to convey a concept can take on very different meanings for different readers. For example, consider the concept of chair. How might the word chair be interpreted by different people? A first grader probably would have a radically different view of the concept of chair than might the chairperson of a department of psychology.

A pre-school child, or one of our special children might need a concept stated in the following way: A chair is used for sitting. For secondary level students we might state the concept thusly: The chair in a committee is the position or individual in that position that is the mediator and administrator of a group of people.

The process of stating the concept in fuller terms allows us to add the sufficient specificity and concreteness to say what we really mean when we are attempting to teach a concept.

We will conclude this section on the inclusion of statements of concepts by saying that the more fully we can develop the statements of concepts and the more appropriately we can relate them to our students, the more easily we can develop the rest of the individualized programs to fit the students' needs.

Example: Suppose we are working with a student who needs help with language skills. The evaluation process (which we have already discussed and which we will again discuss) has given us a rough approximation of what language skills the student possesses and what skills need extra work (or, in some cases, what skills do not exist at all). From this evaluation process, we see that our student cannot recognize and pronounce the combination of letters *ie*. Part of our immediate instruction is sure to try to rectify this problem. In this case, let us write the skill to be learned in the fashion we have mentioned previously.

Our student will recognize and pronounce *ie* when this pair of letters appears by itself or in a word.

The above statement is a fairly explicit statement of the skill we wish to teach. Skills seem to be rather easy to state, so let us now give an example of stating a concept we might wish to teach. Again, the evaluation process has provided us with the kinds of information we need to start preparing instructional goals for our child. We will assume that our hypothetical child has not mastered the concept of plant and that this concept has enough importance to be included in a teaching/learning situation. Our statement would read as follows:

A plant is a living organism that depends on chlorophyll to make its food.

This statement, although greatly simplified from the way a botanist might approach it, is probably appropriate to some early levels of education. Again, the statement, roughly at least, specifies what it is we want to teach.

Values, perhaps the most difficult bits of knowledge to teach, can also be stated in appropriate terms. The evaluation process here will not be as helpful since attitudes and perhaps values change more rapidly than other forms of knowledge. Perhaps interviewing the child will give us the kind of knowledge to know where to start. If we do interview and find out, for instance, that our child despises reading, we may want to teach the following kind of value:

Reading is fun.

The reader will notice that this statement is considerably more ambiguous than the previous one, but we have, at least, set out a statement of the value we want to work towards, regardless of the lack of specificity.

We suggest that some practice in forming statements of what is to be learned would be very useful for the reader. We could continue to provide example after example (some good, some terrible), but we feel that actually making some statements of the kind we demonstrated would be far superior to merely reading about them.

B. Specified Behavioral Objectives

The next step in developing the individualized instruction program is to develop specified behavioral objectives from the statements of what is to be learned. If the reader will refer to the first of this chapter, the process for developing behavioral objectives is fully described. Here, we will only carry further the examples we originally stated for the statements of what was to be learned.

Skill: The student will recognize and correctly pronounce *ie* when seen in words 90 percent of the time in the reading class.

Concept: The student will correctly identify all the plants in the schoolyard and point out where the chlorophyll is visible at a 100 percent accuracy rate.

Value: The student will say that reading is fun. He will indicate this is a true statement by the appropriate mannerisms, e.g., smiling and laughing at the prospect of reading 90 percent of the time.

As we look at these three objectives we see that the objective for the skill we wish to develop has changed the least from the statement of what was to be learned while our objective concerning the value has changed the most. Each of these objectives contain the measurable action verb, the criterion of acceptance, and the conditions under which the behavior must occur. If the reader has followed our prescription and made some statement of what is to be learned it would at this point be appropriate to develop objectives from them.

C. Learning Activities and Materials

Most of us, given the time and proper input, could develop statements of what is to be learned and from these, specify behavioral objectives. As any experienced teacher can tell us, however, teaching and learning are made or broken by the kinds of learning activities and the materials used to enhance the learning. In this section we will try to furnish the reader with some general comments concerning the preparation of learning activities and materials. In such a brief section of one chapter we can only offer generalities. After all, entire books and series of books have been written about learning activities and the materials for learning activities.

The purpose of learning activities, of course, is to help the student incorporate the behavioral changes specified in the objectives into his or her behavioral repertoire. (In simpler terms, to help the students learn whatever it is we want them to learn. You have to excuse our occasional lapses into jargonism, but sometimes we want to say precisely what we mean and only the jargonistic words allow absolutely unambiguous statement.) As Kapfer and Ovard (1972) point out, the most critical factor in developing learning activities is insuring that real learning takes place and not just rote memorization. We are all familiar with occasions in our own learning history wherein we merely memorized material for tests and then forgot the material promptly, once the test was over. This kind of behavior must be avoided. We must try, in as many ways as possible, to foster learning in the form of permanent behavioral changes in our students and not just rote memorization, which amounts only to a short-term behavioral change.

The following four criteria developed from a review of several pertinent sources (see bibliography) should provide the basic guidelines we feel are necessary in preparing the learning activities.

1. The learning activities and the materials used for these activities should allow the student to directly sense (perceive: the idea that has been set forward in the objective). It is necessary to make provisions for the students to hear, smell, touch, taste, feel or read about the idea. If direct contact is not possible, the activities and materials should relate to previous experiences that the student may have had with the concept.

2. The kind of senses that the learning activities and materials employ should relate as closely as possible to the idea in the objective. (In other words, if we are structuring an objective that deals with music, we should try to develop activities that allow the students to hear the music.) By the same token, if we are trying to develop an activity that centers on the texture of the surface of some substance, we should try to incorporate feeling into the learning activity. After all, feeling sandpaper tells one much more than several hundred words spoken to a person about sandpaper.

3. The learning activities should be easily transferable into verbal learning. That is, the experience should help the student

develop the ability to verbalize the experience and relate it in some fashion to past experiences and previous knowledge. Verbalization, either vocal or written, is the only way in which the teacher can be sure such transfer has occurred.

4. The student should be an active participant in the learning experience. As Kapfer and Ovard (1972) state, the student should be involved in making overt responses either verbally or non-verbally.

Meeting these four broad guidelines does not ensure that the learning activity will be either good or successful. Meeting these guidelines, however, will ensure that whatever the learning activity is, regardless of its quality, it will have its usefulness greatly enhanced.

Learning activities are very much like books, movies, and television shows. What is very successful with some people bombs-out completely with others. What works once may continue to be successful or it may never work again. What works with one teacher administering it may not work for anyone else or it may lend to generalizability very well.

The only way we can tell you how to write a "good" learning activity is to practice the business of writing them until you develop a "feel" for doing it. Each teacher will always have successful learning activities and unsuccessful learning activities. Only experience seems to teach us how to maximize our efforts and develop more winners than losers.

Example: Let us take the three objectives we formed from statements of things to be learned earlier in this chapter and develop some learning activities for each of them. After developing each one we will point out how we did or did not comply with the four guidelines stated above.

Skill: The student will recognize and correctly pronounce *ie* when seen in words 90 percent of the time in reading class.

Activity: The student will be presented with a series of words on flash cards and the *ie* in some of them will be pointed out and pronounced correctly by the teacher. The student will then point with his or her finger to the *ie* and pronounce the *ie* until he or she is correct. The teacher will provide prompts initially and fade out these prompts as the student goes through the cards.

Critique: The reader will notice that the activity makes provision for meeting the first of the four guidelines by allowing the student to directly sense the idea (he or she hears it and sees it). The second guideline is followed because the activity relates directly to the objective (the child is actively engaged in identifying and pronouncing the letter group). The third guideline is directly met: the entire activity is built around verbalization. The fourth and last guideline is met with the student actively participating in the exercise.

Whether this learning activity is worthwhile or not can only be determined by the teacher and the student. It may be that this activity is simply terrible.

Concept: The student will correctly identify all the plants in the schoolyard and point out where chlorophyll is visible with a 100 percent accuracy rate.

Activity: The teacher first discusses plants and verbally describes some. Then a film strip identifying plants of the world is viewed by the child followed by the child and teacher walking the school grounds while the teacher asks, while pointing to different objects, "Is this a plant?" The child is to respond yes or no and is further asked to point out the visible chlorophyll. The teacher will provide prompts where necessary.

Critique: This activity, too, meets all four of the guidelines. First, the student directly senses plants and also has two forms of secondary contact with plants (lecture and film strip). Secondly, the activities directly relate to the objective. Third, verbal learning is stressed in the last part of this activity. Fourth, the student is directly involved in responding.

Again, this may be a miserable learning activity. Only trying it out can really give us the information we need to evaluate the activity.

Value: The student will say that reading is fun. He will indicate this is a true statement by the appropriate mannerisms, e.g., smiling and laughing at the prospect of reading, 90 percent of the time.

Activity: The teacher, after determining what topics interest the child, will read stories to the student, stopping frequently to ask questions and elicit responses. The student, further, will be guided in reading stories that are of interest to him or her while the teacher pairs praise and attention with the reading behavior. Reading, further, will be paired with other rewards for good behavior.

Critique: Critiquing an activity designed to teach a value is much more difficult than critiquing other forms of activities. In examining whether or not we meet the four guidelines mentioned above we see that the idea can only be indirectly perceived by the student. The idea that reading is fun cannot be taught directly. (Imagine preparing a lecture or trying to find a film demonstrating how reading is fun.) Second, the senses that would be used in meeting the objective are properly instituted in the activity but there is always the problem of having the child "feel" something. Third, transferring the activities to verbal learning is indirect, i.e., it may or may not occur. Fourth, the student is an active participant and does respond actively.

As can be seen, we really meet only two of the four guidelines completely. One of the guidelines we almost meet, but not quite. Such an activity may or may not be appropriate, but values are very difficult to teach in any manner.

The activities that we developed are, as all human work is, flawed. None of them would be appropriate to all children and most of the readers can find places to disagree with our activities. The point of the matter, however, is that individualized instruction is individualized not only for the student but also for the teacher who prepares the activities. Our purpose, rather, was to demonstrate how objectives can be made to fall in line with our guidelines and how difficult this can be in certain instances. We can only hope that the reader will use the guidelines as general parameters within which to prepare learning activities.

D. Evaluation

In this chapter we have already mentioned evaluation with regard to preparing learning activities. In fact, the emphasis of our book so far has been evaluation. In this section we will examine pre-tests, self-tests, and post-tests.

Evaluation, in the current context, investigates what behaviors are present in the student at the time the evaluation is made. A test is merely an instrument designed to facilitate the evaluation process by measuring whether, in fact, some behaviors exist and to what extent they do exist. We are all familiar with various kinds of tests including multiple choice tests (recognition), true-false tests (recognition), matching tests (recognition and relationships), discussion tests (compare, contrast, name, list, describe, etc.), problem solving tests (construct, solve, etc.), and rote memory tests. Depending on how the objectives for the learning activity are stated, any or all of these may be useful in measuring the amount of change in behavior. Generally, tests should reflect the kinds of verbs stated in the objectives. If the verb "identify" is used, tests stressing "identification" are appropriate and tests stressing "discussion" or "description" are not. Incidentally, the authors are aware of several instructors at all levels that purposely state objectives in one fashion and then test entirely different kinds of functions. They claim that they are maximizing the students' transfer, or that they are just keeping their students on their collective toes. We do not believe that any acceptable rationale exists for mis-testing learning.

In our testing description, we will assume that the reader understands that when we refer to a test, we are referring to a direct assessment of the stated objectives.

Pre-tests

A pre-test is a test given prior to any learning experience dealing with the material on the pre-test. A pre-test, further, provides information to the teacher that can help with the statement of objectives and possible learning experiences.

A pre-test is really part of the process of developing areas of instruction to meet the needs of the student. For example, if we are concerned with whether or not the student can identify certain letter groupings in words and pronounce them correctly, a pre-test will allow identification of which letter groupings, if any, the student has difficulty with. From this information we can formulate statements of things to be learned and the objectives and learning activities to facilitate the learning.

Certainly, if the student has mastered some skills prior to our dealings with the student, there would be little or no need to go through any further process. The pre-test, then, is an instrument that determines what, if anything, in a new area the student must learn.

Self-tests

Self-tests are measuring instruments designed to allow the student to evaluate his own progress within the learning experience. Self-tests may or may not be appropriate at different levels of instruction, e.g., at very elementary levels they may not provide the student with useful forms of input.

Self-tests should be stated and written in the same terms as the post-test, that is, using the same kind of verb form that we ask of the student in the objective.

Post-tests

Post-tests are measuring instruments administered to students after the learning experiences are complete. The post-tests provide the teacher information concerning whether or not the student has learned the new behavior at an acceptable rate, whether he or she can apply new knowledge within the criteria set for acceptance in the objective. There are really two possibilities with the post-test: either the student successfully masters the material and demonstrates this, and hence, moves to new material; or he does not meet the standards for acceptability and new methods must be developed to help the student reach the acceptable level of performance.

Example

Skill: The teacher shows the student forty flash cards, thirty of which contain *ie*. To successfully meet the criteria of the objectives stated previously, the student must correctly identify and pronounce 27 of the 30 *ie*'s, or make less than 3 errors in words containing no *ie*'s.

Concept: The student, walking in the schoolyard, is asked to identify all the plants and show where the chlorophyll is visible. He or she must do so correctly for all the plants.

Value: The student, when presented with the opportunity of reading, will demonstrate that it is fun by smiling or laughing ninety percent of the time such opportunities occur.

Summary

In this chapter we described the development of individualized instruction. There are four basic components in individualized instruction. There are specific behavior objectives, statements of what is about to be learned, learning activities, and tests to measure the occurrence of learning.

Objectives have three basic components: action verbs describing the end result of the learning, criteria for acceptable performances, and the conditions under which the behavior must occur.

Statements of what is to be learned are important in removing ambiguity and providing jumping off places for objectives. The learning activities should fall within four guidelines where possible. These are: close relation of the sense used in the activity to the learning that is to occur, direct sensing of what is to be learned, active responding on the part of the student and transfer to verbal learning.

Three kinds of tests are generally used in individualized instruction, pre-tests, self-tests, and post-tests. The pre-test provides input for the structures of learning objectives and activities. Self-testing provides the student with input concerning his or her rate and accuracy of learning, while post-testing provides the final assessment of whether the learning has occurred at an acceptable rate.

A Final Comment

This chapter is only an introduction into the area of individualized instruction. There are many questions we did not answer and even more that we did not raise. Our hope is that we have provided the impetus for the reader to enter into the study and development of individualized instruction on a far wider base than we could provide.

Chapter **7**

Responsibilities of the University: Making It Work

THE UNIVERSITY has several distinct responsibilities for the learning-disabled child. Some deal directly with the treatment of the disabilities, others precede that step. In most communities universities have five distinct responsibilities. We will sketch all of them while special emphasis will be placed on university training and the role of professional educators as sources in working with the learning-disabled.

1. The university is responsible for training teachers, counselors, psychologists, and other individuals that will be engaged in working with the learning-disabled child.

2. The university should function as a resource center for the community providing academic materials, e.g., professional journals, reference texts, films, and tapes.

3. The university should be a source for professionally trained individuals either on a consultative or volunteer basis.

4. The university should provide the intellectual impetus for learning-situations for the staff of public schools engaged in working with the learning-disabled, e.g., seminars, workshops, dialogues, and other forms of information dissemination.

5. Many universities are able to provide clinics wherein their students gain supervised experience working with the learning-disabled, while the children that attend the clinics benefit from intense, individual therapy.

Training Professionals

The training of professional people to allow them to enter the helping professions (including education) is the most obvious but most difficult of the responsibilities of a university. Universities at the undergraduate level are under state and national constraints to provide a general education with a major in one area or another. Generally the students have a well-rounded general education upon leaving a university, but the specialized professional education curriculum may be an entirely different matter.

Education majors, elementary or secondary, are required at many universities to take philosophy of education, history of education, and the sociology of education. These courses generally appear in one quarter or semester. We do not discredit the usefulness of the knowledge of these areas but we feel that one semester is a rather brief period of time to teach any really useful skills in these areas. The remainder of the course work in professional education generally consists of an introduction to education, audio-visual methods, a couple of teaching methods courses, some educational psychology, and finally, student teaching.

We feel that these courses, generally, do not provide enough training for most teachers. There is argument for the inclusion of each of the aforementioned courses and we do not suggest the deletion of them. What we do suggest is the lengthening of an education curriculum to a five-year program rather than the current four-year program.

A five-year program would allow inclusion of sorely needed training in counseling techniques and counseling practicums, classroom behavior management and classroom guidance, teaching practicums before student teaching, identification of learning disabilities, and school referrals and sources of help outside the schools. We realize that this brief sketch of the needs we perceive for teachers in "normal" schools is not all-inclusive or a cure-all for education's ills. It is, however, a step in the right direction.

Those of us who have attended universities are likely to remember a phenomenon that should definitely be eradicated, one that is closely linked to the curriculum and attitudes surrounding many departments of education. Education seems to be the dumping ground for students who either have failed out of other programs or who have had difficulty with other curriculums. This phenomenon has resulted in a dim view of education students, justified or not, by other college educated people. Joe Blow, who has not done very well in engineering, changes his major to education. This way he can obtain an "easy" degree and satisfy the demands of his parents. At least he will be college educated. If you have had experience at a university, you will also, no doubt, remember that most of the education students would have done quite well elsewhere and that the reputation of academic ease is not particularly well founded.

Why should education suffer from this phenomenon? We feel that it should not. We feel that the requirements for admission to a program in professional education should be as rigorous as any other department and perhaps more rigorous. Educators, after all, are those people who will, in large part, shape the lives of our children and our children's children. We feel that we are justified in exhorting universities to toughen requirements for admittance to and exit from an undergraduate program in education. These requirements must not only be academic, but personal as well. Prospective educators should be subject to the same scrutiny as prospective psychologists or other members of the helping professions. After all, a teacher may reach 150 students a year over a period of 30 years or more. What could be more important than having the best possible people in such important and demanding positions?

Teaching, in recent years, has slipped from a well-respected profession to just another 8-3 job. There are far too many reasons for this reversal to go into here. The current writers believe, however, that a rigorous, well-designed, and revamped curriculum will do much to enhance the image of teacher training. It has, we feel, become a matter of great national importance to up-grade the training of our educators.

A Revised Teacher Education Curriculum

Earlier in this chapter we mentioned our belief that changes are needed in the undergraduate curriculum for teacher education. In order to jog your memories, let us first present a general example of current curriculums and discuss it.[1]

Freshman Year

English Composition
American History
Physical Education
Science

Courses in art, music, geography, library science and an introduction to education.

Sophomore Year

Literature
Mathematics
Physical Education
Health

Courses in world history, sociology, developmental psychology, history of education and educational psychology.

Junior Year

2 years of courses in "minor" area begun: history, chemistry, etc., continued during the senior year. "Methods" courses, courses in music, health, history, school organization and administration, curriculum development, measurement and evaluation.

Senior Year

Courses in speech, science, science teaching methods, courses in the minor area of study, school and community relations, psychology, and student teaching.

This outline is a general one that reflects what the predominant line of thought is in dealing with teacher education. In examining the freshman year, we can find very little to dispute concerning the necessity of including the courses we have compiled as most often mentioned in current college catalogs.

[1]We wish to thank the graduate students enrolled in Educational Psychology 536 during the Summer session at Tennessee State University for exhaustively investigating the curriculums in teacher education at several different universities. The above is a result of their compilations.

The sophomore year, again, is chock full of experiences that should be shared by all college students with the exception, perhaps, of the history of education. (Do you remember Clifford Beers?).

The junior year begins with the students enrolled in a minor area. The minor area generally constitutes the area that secondary school teachers will emphasize in order to gain certification, e.g., history, chemistry, physics, or mathematics.

Courses also appear that are labeled "methods" courses. These courses generally consist of how to teach some subject area, e.g., methods in teaching mathematics, methods in teaching science, methods in teaching English, etc. (Both the authors have had the dubious distinction of having suffered through such courses.) It turns out that the teaching of science, for instance, amounts to teaching just the way you have been taught. Seriously, how many ways can you teach Shakespeare? You can lecture; you can play Socrates; you can show a film; you can assign readings; you can develop special projects; and you can have group discussions. This can be determined by merely thinking about how you might teach something and we doubt that an entire course devoted to teaching the obvious is necessary or useful. These courses, too, very seldom provide opportunity for real teaching experience. Instead you can hear lectures on how to teach something. Many good instructors are involved in these kinds of courses, but there is just so much they can do within the prescribed limits of the course requirements. Our "redundance of the obvious" award goes to the initiator of such courses.

Courses in music, health, and history are carried over from the basic two years and appear during this year also. Course experience in school organization and administration (everyone should know who the janitor must answer to), curriculum development, and measurement and evaluation are final components of the junior year.

The senior year contains courses in speech, science, more "methods" courses, school and community relations (become good friends with the members of the local school board and your troubles are over), some area of psychology (Sigmund Freud was a Taurus), the minor area again, and student teaching.

There are obvious strong points to such a program. It is a very broad and very general program that allows the student a broad spectrum of experiences, and, hopefully, provides educational enrichment in all these areas. Secondly, the program is well defined and structured, giving the student a definite orientation in terms of personal standing with respect to requirements for graduation. Third, the program is tried and tested. We are all familiar with the product of such a program and few question marks exist as to the process and product of the program. Fourth, considerable flexibility is available. Students may choose minor areas, specific "methods" courses (you can actually find out that you can lecture about chemistry, English, history, physics, ad absurdum), and electives in the areas of education and psychology. Lastly, the program has produced adequate, excellent, and superb teachers in the past.

As with all things, however, changes occur. The current needs of education have outstripped the training we have traditionally provided teachers. In examining traditional teacher-training curricula, we can see that no experiences are available ("are required" would be more appropriate since the majority of universities offer a wide variety of pertinent courses as electives on both the undergraduate and graduate level) in diagnosing learning handicaps, diagnosing emotional handicaps, or diagnosing physical problems that will effect learning. Well, ... so what? As you may have noticed throughout this text, we have been emphasizing the identification, diagnosis, and remediation of problems that detract from students achieving all that they can achieve. Providing teachers with knowledge and experience in the identification and diagnosis of problems related to teaching can only enhance the process of continued assessment and placement. Further, teachers will be given the professional leverage via educational experiences to further validate their already accurate conceptions of students who need special help. Teachers would then be "professionally qualified" to initiate referral procedures and would lose the stigma of "getting rid" of problem students. Training in identifying and diagnosing learning impediments, also, considerably eases the referral process by shortening the referral and identification process. This is a benefit both to students and to the school, and provides teachers with the kind of skills to aid in the mainstreaming process. Incidental to the actual functions of teachers, the teacher's professional standing should be considerably enhanced.

Traditional teacher-training has also overlooked the problems of behavior management in the classroom (sometimes referred to by the ambiguous phrase, "classroom discipline"). We suppose that many of us are still operating on the "teachers-are-born—not-made" principle, and assume that no such training as classroom behavior management is necessary. Unfortunately, these kinds of ideas are not congruent to what actually goes on in the real old nasty educational world outside of our nice, secure, and comfortably-removed college settings.

Misbehavior has always been a concern of teachers and administrators but in recent years, misbehavior has grown to include serious behavior problems (beatings, stabbings, arson, and other forms of nasty behaviors). Interracial problems, formerly ignored, are now evident in many settings and just plain old apathy (often referred to as "lack of motivation") is also still present in force.

We doubt that we need to list all the possible kinds of less than desirable behaviors that are apt to occur from time to time to convince you, the reader, that a problem definitely exists. Luckily, not all teachers, or even a large minority of teachers, are faced with severe behavior problems. Even so, training and experience in behavior management can only enhance the teacher's performance.

Courses in classroom behavior management have existed for several years and have just recently gained in popularity (Glover and Gary, 1975). We feel that both theoretical study and training in practical application are necessary components of any complete teacher training curriculum. The advantages of appropriate teacher training in behavior management seem to be many fold. Teachers will be prepared to deal with many kinds of behavior problems from apathy to aggression; teachers will be able to formulate the best possible environmental and personal contingencies in the classroom (given whatever the overall circumstances are) to facilitate learning; and teachers will greatly ease the load of administrators and other school personnel in dealing with behavior problems. Again, in incidental fashion, the professional prestige of teachers should be enhanced by providing "professional qualifications" previously restricted to administrative personnel and guidance personnel.

Traditional teacher-education programs also seldom include courses or experiences in group or individual counseling. Certainly one of the major functions of a teacher is counseling students. This may not be performed in a formal fashion; in fact, the greatest advantage teachers have in a counseling situation is the high degree of informality and trust that is present for the student to initiate the counseling in the first place (Roberts, 1973). All teachers counsel students from time to time. Some teachers are more comfortable than others in a counseling situation, but it is extremely hard to deny that counseling skills can often aid the teacher and the student.

A course in student counseling with some practical experience as one of the components of the course would, we feel, enhance the skills of teachers. Such experiences would provide teachers with the basic skills and a theoretical background for an empathic relationship with students. Individual-counseling skills would certainly facilitate the remediation of behavior problems in the class, add to the dimension of the status of the relationship between the teacher and the students, help open lines of communication with the students, and help develop growth in the students as persons (Tolbert, 1972). (We are aware that considering students as "people" is highly threatening to some of our colleagues, but we recommend it as an illuminating experience and a very satisfying one at that.)

Group-counseling skills, of course, will facilitate the development of a collection of individuals into a functioning group of persons. Group-counseling skills should be of considerable help in dealing with problems shared by a group of students and enhance the development of interpersonal relationships between people (Glasser, 1969). Group-counseling techniques are also useful in facilitating personal growth in terms of self-understanding and acceptance of self. We could probably go on and on about the need for teachers to develop skills in counseling. The most telling argument might have appeared in a recent survey which demonstrated that teachers spent less than one percent of their time meeting their students' needs. Such skills as counseling are within the grasp of teachers already and, with refinement, would add considerably to the repertoire of techniques in the teachers' grab-bag of skills.

Related only in a general fashion to the three needs we described above is the idea that teachers need the skills that will allow them to develop their own curricula, to write effective learning activity packages, and to write specific educational objectives for students. The need for these kinds of skills should be self-evident. As we pointed out in chapter 6, the preparation of learning materials to meet the needs of students becomes the teacher's responsibility. Certainly courses designed to teach such skills already exist, at least on the graduate level in many universities. Someone must know how to teach such skills (after all, people like us begin to prepare our own material and begin to write our own texts). It seems to be a matter here of adapting already existing skills and areas of instruction to produce a good undergraduate experience.

Our last recommendation is that prospective teachers be provided with concrete experience in teaching prior to the last year the student is in school. Many colleges and universities are already moving in this direction by providing some exposure to the classroom for the prospective teachers. Why should students of the teaching profession be expected to teach until they have finished all their formal training? (This is the kind of thinking that results in fuel shortages and Custer's stand at Little Big Horn.) Well, first of all, to see if they like it. There is nothing more miserable than a teacher that hates his or her profession and feels as though all those years in college were a waste of time. (How many former education majors do you know that sell insurance or sell used cars? This is no reflection on the value of these alternate professions, but it certainly is part of the current disaffection with the teaching profession and it should be remedied. Complete remediation of the problem non-satisfying professions is impossible but something must be done to reduce the size of this problem in education.) Secondly, any major learning-theorist, any educational psychologist, or any current educator, will tell you that practical experience is the single best way to facilitate the learning and application of theories.

Before we move away from the new curriculum and ideas concerning the curriculum, we feel that we need to address ourselves to a question that we brought up earlier in this chapter, that of *screening*. We have already pointed out reasons for the necessity of screening so we will address ourselves here to the *means* by which it can be achieved.

(1) *Throw standardized tests out the window.* Standardized tests measure something but we are not aware of any standardized exam that can possibly measure teaching proficiency, dedication, caring for students, or likelihood of remaining in a profession. These test instruments can, naturally, be used to determine what gaps in knowledge students may or may not have and, hence, what areas to remediate. However, we feel that meeting the general standards of admission to a university on standardized test instruments should be testing enough.

(2) *Psychological assessment.* That teachers should be well balanced emotionally seems to be above question at this point. A thorough psychological screening process should be initiated during the first year of the program. Those students who are found to be psychologically less than stable should not be allowed to proceed in the program until such a time as correction or remediation has been made.

(3) *Field experience*. Through the process of field experience, students should rapidly find out whether or not they want to become a member of the teaching profession. Part of the screening process will certainly be self-administered as those students who find that teaching is not for them drop out. Further, if competencies in teaching are stressed, those students unable to meet certain competencies will either have to develop the competencies or leave the program, much as students unable to pass certain courses must leave other curriculums.

A Proposed Curriculum

Freshman Year

English Composition
American History
Physical Education
A Science

Courses in art, music, geography, library science, seminar in education, and field experience in education during the second semester or third quarter consisting of tutorial services and teacher's aide responsibilities.

Junior Year

Identification, diagnosis and remediation of learning disabilities, classroom behavior management, interviewing and counseling, field experiences with practicums in the course areas mentioned above, and a special practicum in counseling. Courses in minor area, measurement and evaluation, curriculum development.

Sophomore Year

Literature
Mathematics
Physical Education
Health (1 semester)

Courses in world history, developmental psychology, educational psychology, identification and diagnosis of learning-disabilities, field experiences consisting of tutorial services and supervised teaching of selected topics.

Senior Year

Courses in speech, science, science teaching methods, courses in the minor area of study, school and community relations, psychology, and a full year of supervised teaching practicum.

Fifth Year

Group dynamics, counseling techniques, preparation of individualized learning materials, group counseling practicum, seminar in teaching problems, student teaching. (Until such a time as course requirements for education majors can be changed, we feel that it is necessary for a fifth year to be added to the traditional four-year or eight-semester program.)

Of necessity the program we describe above is a longer program than the traditional kinds of programs, and certainly seems to be more rigorous. No one likes the thought of lengthening a program just for the sake of lengthening a program. However, until such a time as state requirements can be changed to delete certain redundant courses, the only alternative which will provide the student with the experience to develop proper skills in teacher education seems to be a longer program.

The Consulting Teacher

Throughout earlier sections of this book we have mentioned an individual necessary to the assessment, placement, and instructional programs in the schools. This individual has been referred to as the consulting teacher. We mentioned that this person should have a wide variety of skills, with components normally limited to guidance counselors, special education teachers, and school psychologists. In our current conceptualization of the duties and responsibilities of the consulting teacher, we feel that training for this position should be an interdisciplinary program at the graduate level for students with prior teaching experience.

The program we will outline below overlaps the ideal program developed earlier for undergraduate teacher education. We would hope that implementation of an undergraduate program similar to the one we developed would allow for greater flexibility in the consulting teacher program, leading to an expanded degree of expertise in specialized areas.

A Proposed Curriculum

Identification, Diagnosis and Remediation of Reading Deficiencies.

Identification, Diagnosis and Remediation of Learning Deficiencies.

Identification, Diagnosis and Remediation of Emotional Deficiencies.

Interviewing and Counseling.

Counseling Techniques.

Individual Counseling Practicum.

Group Dynamics.

Group Counseling Practicum.

Classroom Behavior Management.

Practicum in Behavior Management.

Techniques in Teacher Consultation.

Practicum in Teacher Consultation.

Writing and Developing Individualized Learning Materials.

Selection and Use of Commercial Learning Materials.

Psychometric and Projective Testing Techniques and Evaluation.

Research Methodology.

Statistics and Design.

Internship.

As noted previously, many of the experiences cited above overlap the experiences we feel are necessary for the undergraduate teacher-education program. In the current program (current in the sense that we have just devised it, not in the sense that it exists anywhere) a high degree of emphasis is placed on identification, diagnosis and remediation of problems that impede learning. We have listed three separate courses that, depending on a university's format, may be revised into one or two courses. Schools run on the quarter system may find that three distinct courses will be necessary while schools on the semester system may be able to increase the number of hours of course credit and reduce this to from one to two courses. This same problem will exist in all of our suggested experiences, e.g., three, three credit courses on the quarter system may be subsumed by one six hour credit semester course. These decisions will have to be made at individual centers of study and should reflect maximum attention to the development of competencies rather than expediency which is sometimes the case.

Courses in counseling and counseling techniques, along with a practicum are suggested to develop the teacher's competencies in the area of individual counseling both with students and with other teachers. The consulting teacher will be involved in considerable work with individual students and teachers in a consultative, counseling, and instructional role. These course experiences are designed to facilitate such processes.

Since the consulting teacher will frequently be involved with groups of students with similar needs, and with helping to adjust the regular classroom to his or her visits, group counseling and group dynamics skills are definitely necessary. One of the prime functions of the consulting teacher will be conducting the consultation in a manner that will not disrupt the normal class, call special attention to the students in need of the consulting teacher, or cause hostility toward, or resentment of, the children in need of special help. To meet the needs of these very real problems, we feel that these group experiences should help considerably. It has been demonstrated that such group function problems can be overcome.[1]

In line with the prevention of interpersonal and group problems that could easily arise from the consulting teacher's role, classroom behavior management training seems to be a necessity. Such training should facilitate consultation with the regular classroom teacher, managing the regular classroom, and managing the behavior of students in need of special help. Certainly, specific kinds of contingencies can be developed to deal with various

---

[1]Special thanks to Roosevelt Reese and Wiley Shepard for their time in dealing with the group problems involved in the consulting-teacher process.

behavioral problems that may arise in consulting situations.

We have mentioned teacher consultation throughout this discussion and feel that some training is necessary as is a practicum experience in developing skills as a consultant. This kind of experience would, of necessity, combine skills in personnel management counseling and human relations.

Training in writing and developing individualized learning-materials seems to be a very necessary part of the training process of the consulting teacher as would the training in the use of proper commercial materials in individualized instruction. Such experience would have to stress assessment, evaluation, writing skills, and analysis skills. Such courses, as yet, are in experimental stages so considerable thought should be given to developing the appropriate experiences and considerable weight given to actual experiences.

A course experience in psychological testing, at this point, also seems to be a necessary part of the training experience of a consulting teacher. Such an individual should be capable of administering and appropriately interpreting the results of many of these different psychological assessment devices. Emphasis on psychological testing may be reduced in the future, but current practices point to the need for training in this area.

Research methodology, statistics and design are the last skill areas that we feel are absolutely mandatory for the consulting teacher. Research tools are vital to any assessment process, not only assessing one child's growth but in assessing the performance of a total school program. We do not expect that the consulting teacher will be called upon to develop research designs for entire systems, but they should have the knowledge to allow them to participate in such research and adapt new research findings to educational practice in the classroom. Effective, new techniques should not be unused simply because no one can properly interpret the literature.

Throughout the structure of the consulting-teacher curriculum we have emphasized practicum experiences. Our feeling is that theory and facts can only be properly learned and developed if actual practice is provided. (We can also guarantee that the real, live problems of the classroom are seldom as simple as those we discuss in the college classroom.) To take this practicum to its logical conclusion, we feel that a full-time, supervised, quarter-length internship is a necessity. During this period of time the student is field-tested while he or she still has the university faculty to fall back on in case of unforseen problems.

A not incidental problem here is the informal "rank" of the consulting teacher. As most of us can testify, principals outrank school psychologists, school psychologists outrank school social workers, school social workers outrank guidance counselors, and guidance counselors outrank teachers. This may not always be the case but our experience has certainly proved this ranking business out. Well, we "ivory-tower" dwellers will have little, if any, control over the informal ranking of the consulting teacher and his or her associates, but feel that the extensive training should result in an educational specialist degree, which is one step above the counselor, psychologist, social worker level of training. We feel that a consulting teacher must have the informal power to get things done. (For a full discussion of informal structure see A.L. Gary's *Two Years As A Change Agent*.)

The consulting teacher is a necessary part of the school system's whole service programs and, in years to come, will become a more and more important person in the schools.

Special Education

Special education, that field that prepares prospective educators of the learning disabled, has been and is the branch of educator preparation that has done the most for the preparation of their students as professional educators. The course work tends to be far more rigorous than in elementary or secondary education. The emphasis, too, is different. Most universities require in excess of 100 hours of practical clinical work in addition to student teaching. Special education programs are now very nearly five-year programs and represent the best efforts of our current university educators in teacher preparation programs.

There is, as always, room for continued improvement in all areas of teacher preparation.

Psychology and Counseling

Training in psychology and counseling is an almost totally graduate-level form of education. Training in these areas varies widely from school to school and within different areas of concentration. Very generally those psychologists that will be working with schools and counselors receive intense training and practicum experience in counseling and therapy but scant attention is paid to the learning-disabled child. The confines of producing a Master's candidate in one year seem to preclude the training of these individuals for work with the learning disabled. Perhaps it will be necessary to re-examine the curriculum with more attention being paid to the diagnosis and treatment of those children that suffer from learning disabilities. Certainly, new areas of specialization can be offered to enrich learning and skills in this area.

The University As a Center for Academic Knowledge, Information, and Professional Techniques

The current economic crunch that colleges and universities find themselves in is reflected in the library and education materials available at centers throughout the campuses. Most public school systems and private individuals, however, are less able to afford the current journals in learning disabilities and educational psychology and certainly not films and tapes. All professional educators, perhaps especially those that deal with the learning disabled, need to keep up with current literature in the area. New techniques, research findings, and other pertinent information is regularly published in the journals or in supplementary texts, films, and tapes.

It seems to these writers, at any rate, that it is the responsibility of the university to make these materials available to professional educators in the community. While many university libraries, either through design or by economic constraint, do not maintain materials pertinent to education, we urge that this be corrected. It would seem that the universities have the responsibility for providing service to professional educators by maintaining these materials, providing access to the materials, and informing the educators of the availability of the materials.

Certainly many knotty problems of students have been attenuated by the application of new methods and techniques as reported in the literature. These written, filmed, and taped materials prepared by experts in the various fields are a source of great potential importance for the professional growth of our educators as well as their students.

This process should also be a reciprocal process. Professional educators form a large group of potential graduate students. They also have considerable influence in the choices that students make concerning their own education. In a way, in light of the current money crunch, the survival of both groups depends in large measure on the continued interrelationships of the two groups. The educators help provide students, and thereby, income for the universities while the universities provide important professional growth services for the educators. This relationship needs to be cultivated by both groups.

The University As A Source For Expert Help

Universities differ as widely as communities do. Some universities have literally dozens of professionally trained experts whose help may be enlisted in dealing with various learning disabilities. Others may have none at all. This is a rather touchy area but we suggest that contacting various individuals at colleges or universities will rapidly provide information concerning the expertise that the individual may possess or the location of appropriate individuals. Our experience has been that psychologists and university-level educators are extremely honest in assessing their own abilities and areas of expertise. We have never encountered a psychologist or university educator that claimed to be something that the person was not.

We have sort of jumped ahead of ourselves as we need to address several important questions before we deal with enlisting the aid of university personnel. As the current writers can testify, a distinction between community service and consultation needs to be made. Some universities employ their faculty with the expectation that they will provide community service through the university at no charge to the community. These services certainly include working with primary and secondary-school personnel as well as with other community agencies. Universities that expect their faculty to provide such services generally provide released time for the faculty to spend with the community agencies. This is salaried as part of their position.

Most universities, however, make no provisions for their faculty to provide community services. Here is where the rub comes in. A professor who is teaching a full course load of 15 hours and chairing graduate research committees will not have the time or incentive to invest in free community services unless the person is an unusual individual indeed. Hence, many of the best trained professionals are not released or reimbursed for community services.

Few school systems can afford the luxury of hiring these professionals on a consultative basis ($100 to $200 a day is not at all unusual) except for really unusual circumstances. Further, few of the professors who work full time at a university can afford to give much of their time or expertise without pay. This brings us to the responsibility we see that universities have of providing released time, for which the professors are salaried. When community service is sanctioned and encouraged by the universities, schools are much more likely to gain the services of well-trained people. This can't be a one-way street, however. Communities should contribute to the universities that part of the salary of the professionals so as to allow the universities to be able to allow and encourage community service. The cost factor has become so prohibitive as to disallow "freebies" without some input. We do feel, though, that much of the talent and knowledge that university faculties possess are underused without community service.

Decisions regarding the reciprocity of public school systems and universities must be made by each individual community so as to benefit both parties.

Who do you choose? How do you enlist the person's aid? What function will the person serve? If the university has provisions for community service, a question that can be answered by calling appropriate Deans or department heads, the selection process should follow. Before an individual is located and approached, however, it is necessary to know what you will expect of that person. In other words, you need to be able to specify what, exactly, the person will be contacted for. We have all too often had people visit us with various problems that were so poorly specified and unorganized that we had no option except to ask the person to return after some thought had been given to the matter.

What can you reasonably expect from an "expert"? That depends a lot on the area of expertise that the expert has and on the person you contact. Generally you can expect help with what you are already doing. Very few experts will take the problem off your hands or take over from you. In severe cases they may, however, agree to work with the child on an individual and regular basis in addition to what you are already doing.

The best way to enlist the aid of an expert is to ask the person if he is willing to help. It will be necessary, of course, to explain the problem and provide all the pertinent information. A word of caution: Engaging an expert in an area of learning disabilities does not mean instant success. What it probably does mean is a new or different approach being brought to bear with greater amount of experience and training. It is a useful approach but not one that is in any way guaranteed to succeed.

Another area that may be more fertile in terms of availability is the enlisting of graduate students via supervised practicums for help in working with students. Graduate students may provide more individual attention and bring to the fore new techniques and methods. The use of graduate students benefits all concerned. The graduate student gains valuable experience, the public schools gain extra help and extra input, the learning disabled student gains from the individual work and the resources of the university. The university gains by enhancing the training of students while you gain by helping your students. Graduate students may or may not need the teacher's guidance. In any event they are a valuable asset to the learning-disabled. They are generally always supervised by doctoral-level professionals from the universities who inevitably lend their input to the situation.

Steps to Follow in Using a Consultant

1. Develop a complete and explicit statement of the problem.

2. Develop a comprehensive background of the problem.

3. Provide a complete list of available resources.

4. Describe techniques currently being used and the personnel carrying out these techniques.

5. Contact personnel involved in the problem and elicit their willingness to work with the consultant.

6. Locate the appropriate consultant and arrive at a fee and a workable schedule.

7. Stay away from philosophical discussions or arguments. (If you cannot live with the philosophy of the person you have found, find another. Such discussions or arguments tend to eat up time and money that could be used for something else.)

8. Come to some agreement as to what the consultant is to do. (If possible devise a specific objective for this person's services.)

9. Learn the techniques used yourself, if possible.

10. Emphasize maximum results for a minimum of time.

11. Remain cordial and patient. You never know when you might need this person's services again.

No-no's in the Consulting Game

1. Do not pressure a person to assist you.

2. Do not cover-over problems.

3. Do not falsify anything.

4. Do not engage a person who does not have expertise in your area.

5. Do not forget to consult other concerned personnel in your situation.

6. Do not forget to decide what the consultant is to do.

7. Leave no ambiguities.

8. Do not expect miracles.

9. Avoid "brain picking" to gather information that you could just as easily obtain from the library.

Providing the Intellectual Impetus

Universities have the responsibility for being the cultural and intellectual center of their communities. The scope of a university should be to provide for the cultural and intellectual growth of the community as a whole. This responsibility certainly includes providing the impetus, facilities, and coordination for professional seminars, brainstorming sessions, workshops, and other similar activities planned to enhance the level of training and skill exhibited by all members of the professional education community.

This sort of activity should benefit both the university and the community. Continuing dialogues should be elicited from such a program. The input from both parties should enhance the university instruction and the teaching of the learning-disabled.

University Clinic

Many universities have one or more clinics adapted for use for one to several forms of learning-disabilities. These clinics are generally operated by specific university departments for a three-fold purpose. They are used to train their own students in clinical techniques for use with learning-disabled children; they are used for the faculty to research improvements in current techniques and devise new ones; and they are used to provide a service for public schools, children, and parents of learning-disabled children.

A university has no real responsibility to provide such a clinic, but the existence of a clinic is a boon to everyone concerned with the learning-disabled.

Generally any children having the particular disability that the clinic works with are eligible either through referral by public school authorities, social agencies, or parents. It certainly seems to be the responsibility of the public school officials to remain on good working terms with the clinic personnel.

The combined five areas of responsibilities of the university seem to provide more than adequate assistance for the parent or teacher. It would seem to be well worth the reader's time to familiarize himself with the potentials that the local university may have.

Chapter 8

Summing Up: What Is and Should Be

IN THIS TEXT we have described the legislation which ensures that all children, regardless of any form of handicap, shall receive appropriate education in a non-discriminatory manner. We have defined the processes of screening and assessment, and contrasted the traditional approaches to these activities with the approaches that are mandated by the new requirements of mainstreaming. We have described the make-up of the multi- disciplinary team that performs the actual processes of screening, assessment, referral, and placement. The roles and credentials of the individuals that form the multi-disciplinary team were outlined and their specific duties were detailed. We have presented a model for how screening, assessment, referral, and placement should work, and exactly what the functions of each individual involved are and contrasted this to the traditional approach. We have also described many of the bureaucratic stumbling blocks to the process. Special emphasis was given to the development of individualized instruction which is a necessity in the mainstreaming process and we provided very specific examples of such instruction. Lastly we have examined the responsibilities of the universities by examining their methods of training those individuals who must be involved in the educational system and by examining other services they should be providing.

We have, we feel, given a fair representation of what is and what should be. The purpose of this last chapter is to reflect on the educational process in general and examine *how we may bring about change*. The responsibilities of the university are clear-cut. The university must be the focal point of the change. The university trains all the people involved in our educational system. To bring about changes in education that will result in truly equal educational opportunities for our children, we must change how our school personnel are trained and change their interactions with each other. After all, without appropriate training, no amount of legislation is going to bring about change. A tenured teacher, for example, that has never been taught the process of individualizing instruction cannot be expected to individualize instruction on order. The same kind of training problems exist for all other school personnel. To change what goes on in the schools, we must change the people that work in the schools. A legislative decree without provision for such changes in training will result in superficial changes only.

Once the training of school personnel has been made appropriate to the tasks we expect them to carry out, the change in the schools becomes a matter of retraining old personnel. School personnel who have been in the schools for twenty years cannot be made to suffer financially or professionally by changes we ask of them. They must have the training necessary made available to them without causing them to lose their salaries or lose their professional standing. Such training, whether it is done through a leave of absence for university training, intensive in-service work, or additional training during the school year at the university must be beneficial to the person in ways that are more than "furthering your knowledge." Some personal benefit must accrue to these people to make them willing to work very hard to gain new knowledge and skills. Promotions, paid leaves of absence and reimbursed course costs are among the techniques that may work.

When we have changed how the university trains prospective school personnel and have changed the procedures for retraining current school personnel, we must then deal with the logistic problems in implementing the process on two fronts. The first logistic problem is obtaining the necessary equipment, materials, personnel and space for the mainstreaming program. This means additional monies for purchasing and hiring. The second logistic problem is the removal of incompetent personnel. As abhorrent as it may be to deal with this topic, we must come to grips with the fact that there are currently incompetent people within the schools and that any major change of the type this book details will result in people who cannot or will not make the necessary transitions. In 1975, more than 150,000 people trained in education could not obtain employment in the schools. We train, and probably will continue to train more people in education than there are openings for. The reasons for this are complex and will be addressed below, but our current point is that education should not be a place where incompetence or apathy can be tolerated. The pool of people to replace incompetents is large. This problem of incompetence goes directly against the grain of many things designed to protect teachers and other school personnel from political upheaval, particularly tenure. To deal with this problem we must attack some of the "sacred cows" of the educational system and it will not be easy.

Education in the United States is a highly politicized arena. Changes in educational practices are most closely tied to two things: legislation and funding. Of the two, funding is the most important. Other things such as the development of new and better approaches to teaching or scientific breakthroughs in learning take a back seat to the almighty dollar. The kinds of changes that must occur for mainstreaming to be effective can only be implemented by increased state and federal expenditures at three levels, the university, the schools, and the personnel within the schools. Who pays for these increased expenditures? We do. The taxpayers. Why are such increases needed? We will outline the needed changes in expenditures at each of three levels.

The University

To change the kind of training that all prospective school personnel receive, several things must be considered. (1) Changes in courses or learning experiences incur increased costs because new materials must be developed while older ones must be discarded. (2) Increased emphasis on practical skills means a lower instructor to student ratio resulting in an increase in the university faculty. (3) Placement of students within "real" school settings means costs for travel and communications. (4) Increased work or increased learning activities means more faculty. (5) Stricter admission policies will mean fewer students at the general or lower levels and this results in lower funding by student fees and the matching funds from state governments. (6) Increased individualization of instruction will result in a greater need for materials and secretarial help. (7) Additional training may be necessary for tenured faculty resulting in costs for training and for replacing faculty on leaves of absence. (8) Consultative services, workshops, seminars, and other forms of helping services such as clinics and resource centers will have to be funded.

Essentially what we are saying is that if new services are expected of the university, it will be impossible to offer these services without additional funding. The old cliche of "cutting the fat" from higher education is, by and large, so much hogwash. The great majority of publicly supported universities have no "fat" to cut; they are operating at the limit of their current finances.

The School

Changes that must be made within the school are as drastic as those within the university. (1) There will have to be dramatic increases in personnel and these personnel will be entering at higher levels of training. More personnel and more highly qualified personnel mean more money. (2) Provisions for the space necessary to provide the required functions of the school must be made. This means funding for expansion or, at the least, redesign. (3) Equipment and apparatus for the mainstreaming process must be purchased. (4) Individualized instruction will result in greater costs for learning materials purchased commercially and for teacher generated materials. (5) Resource centers, duplication centers and clerical help will have to be increased. (6) Time will have to be released for multidisciplinary meetings and home visits resulting in a still larger staff. In the schools as in the universities, new programs cost money.

Persons within the Schools

Increased expenditure for school personnel falls within four categories, one of which we have mentioned. (1) Increased staff sizes and increased training levels of personnel incur more costs. (2) Pay for leaves of absence will be increased. (3) Reimbursement for additional education must be provided. (4) Costs of in-service training must be provided.

These increased costs must come from tax revenues and here is the problem. Increased taxes for education are highly unpopular. Representatives would have to have almost suicidal tendencies to urge increased taxation. Why? The why is because the voters will almost universally vote against increased taxes and the representatives would not be re-elected. Increasing taxes amounts to spendable income taken away from the people and very few people appreciate this, especially those without children. Most representatives attempt to reflect very closely what the desires of their constituency are. Until people want quality education more than they want to save tax monies, we will not have quality education. It is nearly that simple. All the legislation and court decisions in the world can be made and they will have no effect unless funds are provided to implement them. Until such a time exists when people are educated to see our children's needs, we will not have change.

Lobby Power

In addition to the staggering problem of funding is the problem of power wielded by various groups of persons within our political system. We noted earlier that one of the problems in changing our educational system is the problem of replacing tenured personnel within the system that are incompetent. This will be very difficult to do because of the power of various educational organizations or unions throughout the country. Their position is clear and highly important. No person should ever have his or her job threatened by political whims or changes in the elected officials in some system. Teachers must have the security of intellectual freedom and must be free from fearing for their jobs. This is what tenure is all about. The groups supporting this position are power-ful enough so that we cannot likely expect any change unless the general populace clamors for it. Again this means educating the voter.

We do not believe that tenure should be abolished, rather it should be modified so as to provide incentive for continuing improvement of skills, continued competency. This could be accomplished by re-negotiable five-year tenure contracts wherein a person is continuously granted tenure for five years every year he or she measures up to the competencies necessary for the survival of the schools.

There are other issues that the national educational organiza-tions do not agree on that we believe must be a part of main-streaming. Equitable agreements must be made with these groups that ensure not only their rights but also the rights of our children.

Attitudes Toward Education

We noted that in excess of 150,000 persons qualified to teach during 1975 were not able to obtain positions in the teaching pro-fession. On the face of it, the answer appears simple. We just train too many teachers. Why not "cut down" the number of people we train to better reflect the job market? There are two basic reasons why we do not "cut down". First, teaching, as with all professions, is cyclical in its needs for new members, changing to meet changes in birthrate and educational priorities. It has only been in the last ten years or so that enough teachers have been trained to fill all the open positions. The problem becomes more complex when we consider that some areas of teaching (notably physical education, English and the social sciences) are glutted with well-trained people while other areas (physics, chemistry) still have more openings than qualified people. This same trend also exists at the graduate level where we have far too many guidance coun-selors than currently available positions while jobs in school social work and school psychology remain unfilled. If everyone in educa-tion were trained in the "right" areas, we would have a much healthier job market.

The second reason for this overabundance of teachers and the chronic problem of too many people qualified in the "wrong" areas is one of the "sacred cows" we will have to eliminate. A degree in education is easier to obtain than a degree in nuclear physics. Few educators like to admit this fact but many students who are not succeeding in other curriculums change to a curriculum in education. Within education some areas of specialization are thought to be "easier" than others. Physics, chemistry, and sciences in general are considered the "hard" curriculums while some of the others are considered "easy". It does not take a great flash of insight to see that a person who desperately wants a degree, any degree, will choose what he or she perceives to be the path of least resistance. The result is a high number of people in education who want a degree and have chosen education because they believe it to be less rigorous than other curriculums.

Part of this perceived "easiness" stems from the attitudes of professional educators at the universities in education. Courses in education are inevitably more humane and more closely aligned to meeting students' needs. Whereas in an organic chemistry lecture, for example, 100 students are lectured to and no provision is made for individuality (the emphasis is on rigor), in education courses the emphasis in on treating each person as a human being and structuring the students' experiences so as to maximize learning. There is absolutely nothing wrong with this attitude, most departments could benefit by such an approach, but the result of this successful approach is that many students are attracted by the approach and they tend to avoid course work in areas that are like the areas they left (chemistry, physics).

Attitudes, however appropriate to real teaching, are not the sole source of the problem. Poor guidance and a lack of strenuous screening for prospective teachers and other professions within education cause most of this problem. We will not begin to change our techniques and upgrade the rigor of our education curriculums until the American people decide that we must do so.

We have previously discussed at length the decline in the image of the professional educator in the United States. This image can only be returned to its appropriate place by upgrading our screening and training procedures and by changing our concept of competency within the schools.

Those things that the people of this country believe are important are done within the educational system as a result of their votes. For mainstreaming to be a workable idea, the political climate must be just right or we will end up with another in a series of partial changes that benefit no one. Lastly, it is the responsibility, not only of every parent, but of every American to actively support progressive educational change. *More than 20 percent of all 18-year-olds are functionally illiterate.* This and other equally severe educational problems will remain unsolved until the American population decides to change it. We have the technology, knowledge and ability to drastically improve our educational practices. The American people must decide to do so. Oh, we give such problems lip service. But we are not concerned enough to do what is necessary to bring about change. As long as our own children are not effected, we go on our way and remark, "How horrible. Education must get better." Education will not get better until we become concerned enough to actively seek changes.

Parting Comment

We have not, by any means, given a thorough analysis of the concept of mainstreaming but we have, we feel, summarized it and what it can do and how we must go about implementing it. We urge the interested reader to pursue the topic. Our bibliography provides a good starting point.

Bibliography

Cremin, L.A. *The transformation of the school: progressivism in American education.* New York: Vintage Books, 1961.

Drumheller, S.J. *Handbook of curriculum design for individualized instruction. A systems approach.* Englewood Cliffs, New Jersey, Educational Technology Publications, 1971.

Gibbons, M. *Individualized instruction: a descriptive analysis.* New York: Teachers College Press, 1971.

Gleason, G.T. (ed.) *The theory and nature of independent learning: a symposium.* Scranton, Pen.: International Textbook Company, 1967.

Kapfer, P.G. and Ovard, G.F. *Preparing and using individualized learning packages for ungraded, continuous progress education.* Englewood Cliffs, New Jersey: Educational Technology Publications, 1972.

Mager, R.F. *Preparing instructional objectives.* Palo Alto, California: Fearson Publishers, 1962.

Perkins, H.O. *Human development and learning.* Belmont, California: Wadsworth, 1972.

Williams, R.L. and Anadam, K. *Cooperative classroom management.* Columbus, Ohio: Merrill, 1973.

INDEX

130   2278